# MAKING WINES LIKE THOSE YOU BUY

**by BRYAN ACTON and PETER DUNCAN**

*HOW TO SIMULATE THE MOST POPULAR WINES,
APERITIFS AND LIQUEURS OF THE CONTINENT –
USING EASILY OBTAINED INGREDIENTS*

**ARGUS BOOKS LIMITED**

SBN 0 900841 03 6

Published by

Amateur Winemaker Publications

Argus Books Limited
Wolsey House,
Wolsey Road,
Hemel Hempstead,
Hertfordshire, HP2 4SS
England

*First Edition: September 1964*
*Second Edition: Twenty-Third Impression September 1980*
*Third Edition: December 1981*
*Second Impression April 1983*
*Third Impression June 1984*
*Fourth Impression January 1985*

Printed in Great Britain by
Standard Press (Andover) Ltd., South Street, Andover, Hampshire
Telephone: Andover 59411

# ILLUSTRATIONS

*From photographs by: Radio Times Hulton Picture Library*

# CONTENTS

*The connoisseur takes his pleasures seriously and with great concentration. A pressmaster of a famous vineyard tastes his new wines.*

# Introducing this book

THOUSANDS make wine, much of it excellent, and many are content just to produce their own country wines – and drink them! But winemaking, like any other worthwhile pursuit, contains an element of challenge, and to the serious winemaker the ultimate challenge is to be able to reproduce from his own resources the famous wine types of the world, at a fraction of their normal cost.

Your true winemaker must gradually become, to however slight a degree, a student of "commercial" wines, and it is inevitable that, gradually, he will wish to make at home wines like those he buys, and loves. He can do it the easiest way of all, of course, by buying one of the many "kits" now on the market, which vary widely both in price and quality. They reduce winemaking to its ultimate simplicity but, as any winemaker knows, they are far more expensive than wine produced from garden or wild fruit, and sometimes nothing like as good. So the easy way is also the expensive way.

"Making Wines Like Those You Buy" tells you in detailed fashion how better to do the job from your own ingredients, with minimal cost and maximum satisfaction.

All recipes are given for either 4.5 litres (1 gal.) or 20 litres (4½ gal.) quantities, since it is felt that many winemakers of experience will prefer the larger quantity.

This book also contains full and comprehensive instructions on the making of LIQUEURS, the production of which at home affords a dramatic economy.

There is no doubt that Bryan Acton and Peter Duncan have between them produced what has become the accepted textbook for these specialised aspects of our enthralling hobby.

C. J. J. BERRY

# CHAPTER I

# Basic Winemaking

THE title of this book–"Making Wines Like Those You Buy" – was deliberately chosen.

There have been a great many books on winemaking since it became such a popular hobby and most of these have been concerned either with the techniques involved or with recipes for Country wines. This little book differs from all these in that it boldly sets out to help produce wines which can compare with those you might drink on the Continent.

Until fairly recently the average person in this country had but little appreciation of the virtues of wine. It is still not uncommon to hear someone say "We had a nice bottle of Port at Christmas time"; a statement which contrasts violently with the amateur winemaker's "I bottled 60 bottles of Elderberry Port last night." The real appreciation of wine came when people started to flock to the Continent for their holidays. They make very poor tea abroad, if at all, and the warm climate no longer makes coffee such a satisfactory thirst quencher. In many places the local water is still suspect so that wine is really the only drink available.

It is good honest wine, litres and litres of it pouring down millions of eager throats in an endless torrent and with very satisfactory results to one's state of contentment. It is curious that with all the sightseeing tours undertaken abroad the only lasting memories are often of friendly cafes with good wine and some music that produced a state of inner peace reached but rarely in life.

# How to afford a bottle of wine a day

We will suppose, dear reader (what a lovely phrase that is! especially as "dear reader" may be a giant of an Australian sheep rearer who just wants cheap "plonk") – we will suppose that you are a wine lover. Why else, indeed, would you be reading this? If you were rich enough you would have a great cellar crammed full of the choicest wines. This is the region of day-dreaming and what pleasanter way of spending an evening than to browse through a wine catalogue (with a glass of wine in one's hand) and to furnish an imaginary cellar with Ports, Madeiras, Sauternes, Clarets and so on? The cost of actually doing this would of course be quite prohibitive for most of us, and when one comes down to earth it is in the cheaper sections of the catalogue that one starts to look. If one cannot afford Montrachet then perhaps Macon Blanc will have to do. But even these are expensive if one wants to drink wine regularly. A bottle of cheap wine a day at £1.90 will run up £700 in the course of a year. Wine kits averaging 40p a bottle will run near £150 a year. What this book offers is a bottle of wine a day for only £50 a year utilizing fruits from the garden and hedgerows.

# But what of the quality?

It is a curious fact that home-made cakes are valued as being much better than bought cakes while the reverse is the case when wines are considered. Unfortunately, in the past, this was indeed the true position. The literary scorn of our "abominable rustic concoctions" was generally justified for only in the realm of Mead, Cider, Beer and Whisky did the inhabitants of these islands excel. For the rest there were off-flavoured Parsnip wines, catty Elder-flower wines and other oversweet cordials far removed from the excellent wines of the Continent.

The impact of science (which is only knowledge, after all!) on winemaking has produced a revolution that has made it possible for wines to be made which resemble those of France, Italy and Germany. Many winemakers using these new techniques still prefer to make country wines and their wines are very much higher in quality than those of their ancestors.

9

# How good are those wines going to be?

An honest answer to this question is that if you pay attention to everything in this book, about 80% of the wines you produce will be as good as the wines you buy in the cheaper ranges of commercial wines and about 10% will be of such excellent quality that they will not be disgraced in the company of more expensive commercial wines. About 10% may be disappointing and we can afford to carry that amount of failures. We do not claim that with the ingredients we use or in the smaller quantities we make we can match the best of commercial wines. Such wines as Chambertin in the Burgundies, Vintage Port, Chateau d'Yquem in the Sauternes, Chateau Latour in the Clarets and the best Hocks and Moselles stand in a class of their own and always will.

However, having said that let us illustrate the point with a story. Former Editor of the "Amateur Winemaker" magazine, Mr. Cyril J. J. Berry, once sent a couple of bottles of his own wine across to some friends in France with whom his daughter Gay was staying. The French friends, themselves extremely knowledgeable about wine, so valued this wine that they rated it as a liqueur and served it to their friends as such on special occasions. That is how good a wine you can make from a mixture of such ingredients as apricots, grape concentrate, elderberries and bananas. Don't be overawed by wine snobs and connoisseurs. The whole purpose of this book is to allow you to make good, honest, everyday wines for your table and for social drinking.

# Basic knowledge

We would like to bring to your notice at this point another book in this series which, if you are a beginner and intensely interested in winemaking, you would do well to acquire. This is **"First Steps in Winemaking"** (from Argus Books Limited, Wolsey House, Wolsey Road, Hemel Hempstead, Herts. HP2 4SS, England). In the present book you are expected to follow recipes blindly in order to achieve results. With the aid of "First Steps in Winemaking" you would get to know the reasons behind the recipes, be able in time to design your own recipes, and in every sense of the word be able to call yourself a "Craftsman in Wine".

10

*Containing all the promise of the future – beauty and wine. Luscious grapes, the raw material of the wines you buy.*

# How wine is made

For those who are just beginning their lifetime of winemaking we will outline in non-technical language just how an alcoholic drink such as wine comes to be made.

Yeasts are some of Nature's "demolition engineers." It is their job to break down vegetable matter into its basic elements so that life can renew itself again from these elements. This is what is happening in a compost heap in the garden or when some fruit salad starts to go "off" in the larder.

However, yeasts can do one thing which human beings cannot do. If our air supply is cut off we die, but if the air supply of yeasts is cut off they can go on living provided a supply of sugar is available. The sugar is broken down by the yeast into alcohol, carbon dioxide gas and energy, the latter being what the yeast requires to live and grow.

All that a winemaker does basically is to take a mixture of sugar and fruit juice (generally diluted with water), add yeast, which is a living organism, and allow the yeast colony to grow with plenty of air, then cut off its air supply and allow the yeast to attack the sugar, producing alcohol. In each gallon of must (the initial sugar/fruit juice mixture) every pound of sugar dissolved will furnish the wine with about 5% alcohol by volume (about 9° proof spirit). Even yeasts cannot go on for ever, and when the alcohol tolerance of the yeast is reached fermentation stops, the yeast dies, and the wine starts to clear and become stable. This is why most yeasts are unable to produce more than 16%–18% alcohol except under rare conditions.

# Why we use mixtures of ingredients

Of all the fruits in the world, the grape is supreme for winemaking. It has (when at its best) the ideal balance of sugar, acid, tannin and so on which can produce a fine balanced wine. In Britain very few, if any, of our fruits and none of our vegetables are as balanced as the grape. However, by blending together a number of ingredients into a composite fruit/vegetable juice mixture we can arrive at a balance which is in most cases as good as that possessed by the grape. If you find that one of the ingredients is not available, try to substitute for it a similar fruit or vegetable, and in this way you will ensure that the balance is maintained.

Ordinary granulated sugar is intended to be used in the wines mentioned in our recipes. There are many other forms of sugar, some with unwanted flavours of their own, but they all behave the same way in the presence of yeast in a well balanced must.

What is important, however, is that sugar should be added to a must in syrup form little by little as indicated in the recipes. In high alcohol wines this allows the yeast to increase its tolerance of alcohol and so the furnished wine is higher in alcohol than it would otherwise be.

Another important point is that when a wine has finished fermenting and has been racked (siphoned off its yeast deposit), no further sugar should be added AT THAT POINT. Otherwise this will tend to produce a very minute continued fermentation which will prevent the wine from clearing rapidly. Wines should be sweetened, if so required, when they are completely stable and not immediately after fermentation.

## Double your money's worth

If you are following one of the recipes for a dessert wine, particularly with fruit such as elderberries, bilberries, plums and damsons, fruits with a great deal of colour, it is sometimes possible to get two wines from the same fruit. One of these is the heavy-bodied dessert wine as per recipe and the other is a light table wine.

In most of these cases the recipe will advocate fermenting on the pulp for a few days after which the pulp is strained off. If at this point the pulp (if sound and holding together well) is placed in another fermenting bin and 900 g (2lb.) sugar per 4.5 litres (1 gal.) and 25 g (¾oz.) acid per 4.5 litres (1 gal.) are added and the liquid content is restored with water at 20°–25°C (70°–75°F), the fermentation will continue. The pulp is now strained off finally a couple of days later and a light table wine of the rosé type will result.

## Equipment

The very minimum of equipment required is:

A polythene 10 litre (2 gal.) bin as a fermenting bin.

A glass jar or demijohn.

A polythene funnel.

A nylon sieve.

A piece of rubber tubing about a yard long.

A piece of glass tubing bent into a small U at one end as a siphon tube.

Additional glass jars or polypins to hold wine in bulk are added as one's winemaking proceeds.

Fermentation locks (devices which allow the carbon dioxide to bubble off while preventing the entry of bacteria) are very useful to beginners since they indicate the speed at which the fermentation is proceeding.

A hydrometer and trial jar are essential once one has started serious winemaking. Details of their use are given on Page 14.

Metal and enamel containers can be used for boiling up ingredients where indicated but should never be used for fermentation as otherwise metallic hazes and perhaps poisons are released into the wine.

# Beginner's "Vin Ordinaire"

We have said earlier that it would be advisable to obtain another book in this series, "First Steps in Winemaking" if you are an absolute beginner. It is always better to know why you are doing things rather than follow recipes blindly. Meantime, however, you want to get on with the winemaking as quickly as possible, and you may not even want to wait long enough to obtain the wine yeasts, nutrients and so on, that appear in later recipes. What you want is a quick trip to the nearest supermarket for one or two ingredients, stopping off at the chemists for some yeast, and straight home to winemaking. While it is not possible to produce a tip-top wine under these conditions, since it will lack certain balancing ingredients and you are unlikely to leave it long enough to mature before drinking it, it should nevertheless compare not unfavourably with the rough local wine you might encounter in French bars. It will in fact be rather stronger in alcohol. We assume you have the basic equipment mentioned, so the ingredients you need are:—

Two 375 g (12 oz.) packets of raisins or sultanas
550 mls (1 pt.) tin of fruit juice (orange, apple or pineapple)
900 g (2 lb.) granulated sugar

14

**1 lemon**

**Some dried yeast (this is sometimes sold in shops in small packets as baker's yeast or Allinson's dried yeast. Do not use brewers yeast or your wine will pick up the flavour).**

*Method:*

1. Boil up the sugar with 570 ml (1 pt.) water for a few minutes until the solution becomes crystal clear. Allow it to cool and store in a bottle for the time being.

2. Wash out your plastic bucket well with plain water.

3. Chop the raisins or put them through a mincer and place them in the bucket.

4. Next add the juice of the lemon, the fruit juice and 570 ml (1 pt.) of the sugar syrup.

5. Boil up 2.85 litres (5 pt.) of water and add them boiling to the bucket. Stir well until everything is well mixed.

6. Cover the bucket with a blanket or piece of polythene and allow it to cool to room temperature (around 20°C (70°F)). This is of the utmost importance for if the yeast is added when the temperature is above 27°C (80°F) it may become seriously weakened.

7. When the must is at room temperature add a teaspoonful of the yeast, stir well and re-cover the bucket, and keep in a temperature of 20–25°C (70–75°F).

8. Look at the must occasionally, without completely uncovering the plastic bucket. When the raisins come up to the surface en masse the fermentation has commenced. This may take a few hours or a few days, so be patient.

9. We will call the day on which fermentation starts Day 1, and the procedure then continues as follows.

Day 1–Day 4. Stir brew twice daily, replacing cover each time.

Day 5. Strain off the wine from the pulp through a nylon sieve into the demijohn jar, add 150 ml (¼ pt.) of the sugar syrup, shake the jar well or stir with the handle of a wooden spoon to mix in the syrup well and then plug the jar with a firm wad of cotton wool.

Day 6. No action.

Day 7. Add 150 ml (¼ pt.) of sugar syrup, stirring in well as before and replace cotton wool plug.

Day 8. No action.

Day 9. Taste wine. Ignore horrible flavour but look for a lack of sweetness. If there is little sweetness apparent add another 150 ml (¼ pt.) of sugar syrup, mix well and replace plug. If the wine still tastes sweet delay the sugar addition for two days.

Day 10 and 11. No action.

Day 12. Repeat the procedure for Day 9. This sugar addition will use up the last of your syrup. Do not be surprised if this last addition cannot be added for several days, since the yeast is reaching the point at which its further growth will be inhibited by the alcohol present. Temperature will also affect the rate of fermentation. Never add any sugar until the yeast has used up that already added or you may be left with an oversweet wine.

The wine should now be left for another fortnight to finish its fermentation, and when it no longer tastes sweet and only a few bubbles are rising to the surface, it has to be racked, i.e. poured off its sediment of yeast and pulp debris. If you have a second demijohn this should be used, but otherwise six wine bottles or other containers should be used. If you have some rubber tubing the wine can be siphoned off carefully so that the siphon tube is not too close to the sediment, otherwise it must be carefully poured. Stop pouring if any sediment starts to flow into the new container and re-plug both jars with cotton wool and wait some hours before continuing pouring. Finally top up the new jar with tap water until it is completely full and plug with a bored cork or a very tight wad of cotton wool. Place jar in a cool place.

10. Have a look at the jar after about a fortnight. If a fine sediment of yeast has formed everything is all right. If on the other hand a thick sediment forms (say over 5 mm (¼ inch) thick) or particularly if a two-tone sediment occurs (light brown yeast and yellowish-green fruit pulp) rack the wine once more and again top up with tap water and re-plug the jar once more.

11. Now you must be patient, neither disturbing the wine nor tasting it for three months.

12. After three months rack the wine and sweeten it up to your own taste with sugar syrup (Normally 150 ml (¼ pt.) or 280 ml (½ pt.) syrup is sufficient – syrup made by boiling 225 g (½ lb.) sugar with 150 ml (¼ pt.) water). You will find that this makes a distinct improvement to the wine, and if it is your first wine you will probably drink it at this stage. It should really be kept another

three months at least. It is not a wine that merits bottling, so fill up your decanters from the jar and Good Health! You have become a winemaker!

# Temperature

While commercial experts still disagree on the optimum temperature for fermentation, it has been found that 20–35°C (70–75°F) is suitable for most purposes. Temperatures of over 27°C (80°F) should be avoided. At very low temperatures the fermentation tends to slow up or even stop. Certain yeasts are designed to operate at low temperatures and will sometimes continue a very slow fermentation in unheated rooms in winter.

## Pectinol or Pectolase

This is an enzyme, obtainable from all winemaking suppliers, which will destroy pectin. Where quoted in recipes it will assist the rapid clarification of certain wines.

## How to prepare a yeast starter

1. Take a clean wine bottle, sterilise it with the stock sulphite solution. (See Page 17).

2. When bottle is sterilised rinse out under tap and plug with cotton wool.

3. Boil up one of the following mixtures in a saucepan (with a lid) and allow to cool (with the lid remaining on):

*Either*  10 ml (1 dessertspoon) Malt Extract
10 ml (1 dessertspoon) sugar
5 ml (½ teaspoonful) citric acid
2 cupfuls water

*Or*  Juice of two oranges
10 ml (1 dessertspoon) sugar
2 cupfuls water

*Or*  1 cupful of the fruit juice which will be fermented
1 cupful water
10 ml (1 dessertspoon) sugar

4. When mixture is at *room temperature* pour into bottle, add yeast and replace cotton wool. Many modern wine yeasts can be added in this way without any prior preparation. Stand in temperature of 25°C (75°C) approx.

5. Agar cultures and liquid yeasts will normally start fermenting in a matter of hours, but some yeasts, in particular dried yeasts, may take several days.

6. A further 24 hours should elapse before adding the culture to the main must if such a wait is possible.

7. If only two-thirds of the culture is added to the must and the starter bottle is topped up with a fresh sterile starter mixture the starter can be used many times before being rejected. In between uses it should be stored in a refrigerator and only brought into the warm some hours before use again.

8. Some of the finest wine yeasts are sold in test-tube form, the yeast being on an agar slant. Many amateur winemakers find difficulty in slipping the agar jelly slant out of the test-tube. An alternative method is to immerse the test-tube in the stock sulphite solution to sterilise the outside of the test-tube, after which it is rinsed under the tap, unplugged and the entire test-tube is dropped into the starter bottle. A slight tilting of the bottle will ensure that the starter mixture fills up the test tube, which can be extracted when the starter is added to the must.

# Using the hydrometer

It would be out of place to give a detailed account of the hydrometer in a book of this nature. We intend therefore to highlight two uses to which it can be put.

The hydrometer is simply a weighted hollow tube containing a graduated scale. It is floated in the wine (which is first poured into a suitable test jar) and the depth to which the hydrometer sinks gives a measure of how much sugar the wine contains.

The beginner's main problem is knowing how much sugar can be added to a fermenting wine, and at what rate. The secret of success is to take hydrometer readings about every two days and to wait until the reading has fallen to 10 (1.010) or below before adding further sugar during the first fortnight of fermentation and then to add it at the rate of 110 g (¼ lb.) per 4.5 litres (1 gal.) each time the

| Specific gravity | Gravity | Weight of sugar | |
| --- | --- | --- | --- |
| | | gms in 4.5 litres | ozs in gallon |
| 1.000 | 0 | 0 | 0 |
| 1.005 | 5 | 28.5 | 1 |
| 1.010 | 10 | 57 | 2 |
| 1.015 | 15 | 113 | 4 |
| 1.020 | 20 | 198 | 7 |
| 1.025 | 25 | 256 | 9 |
| 1.030 | 30 | 340 | 12 |
| 1.035 | 35 | 425 | 15 |
| 1.040 | 40 | 481 | 17 |
| 1.045 | 45 | 538 | 19 |
| 1.050 | 50 | 595 | 21 |
| 1.055 | 55 | 652 | 23 |
| 1.060 | 60 | 708 | 25 |
| 1.065 | 65 | 765 | 27 |
| 1.070 | 70 | 822 | 29 |
| 1.075 | 75 | 878 | 31 |
| 1.080 | 80 | 935 | 33 |
| 1.085 | 85 | 1020 | 36 |
| 1.090 | 90 | 1077 | 38 |
| 1.095 | 95 | 1134 | 40 |
| 1.100 | 100 | 1190 | 42 |
| 1.105 | 105 | 1247 | 44 |
| 1.110 | 110 | 1304 | 46 |
| 1.115 | 115 | 1360 | 48 |
| 1.120 | 120 | 1417 | 50 |
| 1.125 | 125 | 1474 | 52 |
| 1.130 | 130 | 1530 | 54 |
| 1.135 | 135 | 1587 | 56 |
| 1.140 | 140 | | |
| 1.145 | 145 | | |
| 1.150 | 150 | | |
| 1.155 | 155 | | |
| 1.160 | 160 | | |

reading falls to the 10 mark. If sugar syrup is made up as instructed in the recipes each 150 ml (¼ pt.) syrup contains 110 g (¼ lb.) sugar.

After about a fortnight the reading can be allowed to go down to the 0 mark (1.000) or below before more sugar syrup is added.

The second problem, that of ascertaining how much alcohol a wine contains, is a little more complicated. There is no method of doing this which is at the same time both easy and accurate.

The following method gives a fairly close approximation and is about the simplest to use, and corrects to a great extent the effect of substances other than sugar dissolved in the must which affect gravity readings. Work wholly in litres or wholly in gallons.

1. Take a gravity reading of your initial must.

2. Read from the table the weight of sugar in 4.5 litres (1 gal.) which corresponds to this gravity.

3. Calculate from this the amount of sugar in the number of litres or gallons you actually have initially (not the number you intend making).

4. Add to this figure all the weight of sugar you add to the must during the course of fermentation (sugar syrup/each 570 ml (1 pt.) equals 450 g (1 lb.) of sugar.)

5. Divide this total of sugar by the number of litres or gallons of finished wine and from the table read back the gravity corresponding to that weight of sugar.

6. Take the gravity of the finished wine and deduct it from the gravity just read.

7. Divide this gravity drop by 7.5. This is the percentage of alcohol by volume in your wine.

8. If you want the figure in degrees of proof spirit multiply the percentage by volume by 1¾ or 7/4.

*An example:*

3.4 litres (¾ gal.) of must of gravity 35 (1.035).

Sugar equivalent 425 g (15½ oz.) per 4.5 litres (1 gal.) from the table multiplied by ¾ gives 319 g (¾ lb.) sugar approx.

1150 ml (2 pt.) of syrup are added in the course of fermentation equalling 900 g (2 lb.) sugar.

Total sugar 1.22 k (2¾ lb.) equalling a gravity of 104 approx. (1.104).

20

(Final volume was 4.5 litres (1 gal.)
Final gravity – 5 (0.995).
Deduct 995 fom 1104 gives a gravity drop of 109.
Divide 109 by 7.5 gives approx. 14.5% alcohol by volume or 25° proof spirit approx.

# Acid

Acid is essential for a balanced fermentation, for the production of flavour during maturing and for its own effect on the palate, without which a wine would taste insipid. Generalising somewhat, a dry wine requires about three parts per thousand acid and a sweet wine about four p.p.t. (expressed in terms of the Continental standard – sulphuric acid – which acid is of course never used itself in winemaking).

The recipes in this book have been worked out to reflect the correct acidity, and also the correct balance of acids where possible, but being recipes they have the fault that they cannot take account of changing climatic conditions. In a very long hot summer the acidity of our native fruits will be below that estimated, while in a very poor "typical English summer" the acidity would be more than estimated.

It is advisable to take a check of the acidity of wine musts and to adjust them to the correct figure. There are on the market very useful "Chemical Wine Testing Kits". These kits test acid content, sugar content, starch hazes and pectin hazes.

The manufacturers claim that it is accurate to within 0.2 p.p.t. It is very easy to use and will ensure that wines are balanced and sound.

# Sulphur Dioxide

Sulphur dioxide has been used in commercial winemaking since time immemorial. Amateur winemakers now use sulphur dioxide also, either in the form of Campden tablets or as potassium metabisulphite or sodium metabisulphite, better known to winemakers simply as sulphite. Campden tablets are the most handy for the winemaker who makes only the occasional gallon of wine, and each tablet represents 50 parts per million (p.p.m.) sulphur dioxide.

More expensive winemaking requires some regard for the cost of subsidiary chemicals used, and it is more economical to purchase 500 g (approx. 1 lb.) sodium metabisulphite through a chemist (cost under 50p) and to make this into a stock solution. The metabisulphite crystals are poured into a gallon jar, about three pints warm water added and the whole shaken until the crystals are dissolved. The jar is then topped up to the gallon mark with cold tap water. The fumes which arise from this solution are the same choking ones which occur in "smog" so care should be taken not to inhale these during mixing or in later use of the solution.

### Some Uses of Sulphite:

1. When a fermentation is started in which no heat or boiling water have been used in the preparation of the must, 100 p.p.m. sulphite should be added per 4.5 litres (1 gal.) of must (2 Campden tablets or 10 mls stock solution). The yeast should be added *24 hours later*. This procedure will kill off or inhibit the activity of harmful bacteria without unduly slowing down yeast activity, and will assist in the production of small amounts of glycerol. In addition the flavouring esters of the ingredients are now contained in the must instead of having been driven off by heat or boiling water.

2. When racking wines, particularly white wines, the racked wine should be treated with 50 p.p.m. $SO_2$ (1 Campden tablet or 5 ml stock solution per 4.5 litres (1 gal.)). This procedure helps to prevent wine from becoming over-oxidised due to too much aeration and ensures better maturing.

Sulphite can be repeated at each racking without any danger of sulphite building up in the wine.

3. The sterilisation of jars, bottles and corks should always be carried out with the aid of sulphite. The stock solution is most satisfactory for this, and about 550 ml (1 pt.) of solution should be put into a separate bottle for this purpose. To sterilise a jar the solution is simply poured into the jar, the jar is swirled around and then the solution is poured back into the bottle once more. 550 ml (1 pt.) of solution, although becoming dis-coloured in its use, will last several months normally and as long as the sulphur dioxide can be smelled the solution remains

active. Bottles are also sterilised in the same way, by pouring the solution from bottle to bottle. Corks are placed in the funnel used at these times and become sterile in the course of bottle sterilisation.

4. The stock solution can be diluted by nine times its own volume to provide a solution that is useful for mopping up spilled wine and large-scale disinfection of the winery.

# Possible troubles

Using the recipes in this book one should but rarely encounter wines which remain persistently hazy even after several months maturing. In compiling the recipes we have avoided using materials which might cause hazes or else have included haze destroying enzymes in the recipe where it has been anticipated hazes might occur.

The following summary of the principal causes, detection and treatment of hazy wines may however be of use on some occasions. It is as well to wait several months before deciding that a wine has a persistent haze.

*Pectin hazes:* These are the commonest. To test, take one volume of wine and add to it four volumes of methylated spirits. Allow to stand for half an hour. If pectin is present jelly-like clots and strings will form. Treat the wine with 15 g (½ oz.) of Pectinol or Pectolaze per 4.5 litres (1 gal.) and bring into a warm room for about a week.

*Starch hazes:* These occur in grain wines and wines made from apples and similar fruits. Test by taking a glassful of wine and adding a few drops of iodine. If starch is present the wine will turn indigo blue. Treat the wine with 15 g (½ oz.) Amylozyme 100 per 4.5 litres (1 gal.) (this latter enzyme preparation can be obtained from most amateur winemaking suppliers), and bring into a warm place.

*Non-depositing yeast hazes:* These are due to single yeast cells which fail to sink to the bottom of the container. There is no reaction to methylated spirits or iodine. They can be removed by filtering or will tend to settle naturally after lengthy maturing.

*Lactic Acid bacteria hazes:* These are revealed by a silky sheen which is seen when the jar is swirled. Sulphiting with 150 p.p.m. $SO_2$ (3 Campden tablets per 4.5 litres (1 gal.)) will clear, although in some cases finings may have to be used.

*Refermentation hazes:* Sometimes a tiny yeast colony re-establishes itself after primary racking and the wine remains cloudy with active yeast cells. These are revealed by the small train of bubbles rising to the surface and by a yeast sediment occurring. The wine should be treated with 100 p.p.m. $SO_2$ (2 Campden tablets per 4.5 litres (1 gal.)), or allowed to complete its fermentation in the normal way if desired.

*General Notes:*

Wines which remain cloudy after the above treatment can be cleared either by fining or by filtration. Finings can be purchased from most suppliers and should be used as instructed on the pack. If the finings fail to work, a small amount of grape tannin or tannic acid should be added to the wine (say 5 ml ¼ – ½ teaspoonful per 4.5 litres (1 gal.)) as finings only work in the presence of tannin. Such an addition may be necessary after fining to restore the astringency required in a wine (white wines mainly).

Filtration should rarely be practised. It spoils more wines than it improves.

# CHAPTER II

# Sherry: Dry, Sweet

The soft warmth of sherry has ushered in many a romantic evening, and has comforted many a weary wanderer over the highways of life. The excellence of this wine, the Spanish would say, is due to the very fine quality of their grapes, and to the techniques employed, particularly that involving the formation of a yeast film or "flor" that gives a unique bouquet and flavour to their dry fino sherries.

Sherry is essentially a fortified white wine produced in a limited area around Jerez de la Frontera, a town in Southern Spain between Seville and Cadiz. The predominant soil of the area is a dazzling white earth known as alberiza, which contains a high proportion of gypsum, and although vines planted on alberiza give smaller yields, the quality of the grapes is considered to be better than those grown on the greater-yielding clay or sandy soils also to be found in this region.

Here in Great Britain a great deal of research has been conducted into sherry production, and indeed it is still going on in research laboratories and by individual winemakers. Enough is now known to be able to produce "sherries" that will satisfy all but the out-and-out sherry connoisseur.

It is not the intention to dig deeply into the background information of sherry production, but rather to concentrate this wisdom into carefully constructed recipes, and to outline a simple technique which will produce the desired results.

First of all it is necessary to give some thought to the selection of suitable ingredients. The illustrious grape has in normal years qualities of balance which few other fruits can even approach. However, once these qualities are known, it is possible to devise combinations of materials which together will come close to matching the high standards set by the grape.

Fruits obviously fulfil more of the desired qualities than other ingredients, but not all fruits are suited for the purpose. Red fruits, for example, contain a great deal of tannin which is not in character with sherry. Again, citrus fruits contain the wrong sort of acid. Such ingredients as yellow plums, greengages, figs, raisins, sultanas and white grape concentrate are very suitable. Their own flavours are often not what is wanted, so that considerable dilution is necessary, and this in turn causes a lack of body.

There are two principal ingredients which can supply body to a wine (other than grains such as wheat or barley which are not suitable because of their nonvinous flavour). These are bananas and parsnips. It must be mentioned here that beetroots would also supply body and lose their colour rapidly, but their earthy flavour tends to persist unless one is prepared to be very patient and mature the wine for a long time.

# Gypsum

Another ingredient which plays a part in sherry-making is calcium sulphate, better known as gypsum or plaster of Paris. Not only does gypsum form part of the soil of Jerez; it is also scattered over the grapes before pressing. It has the effect of increasing the acidity of the must, but at the same time appears to play a part in sherry flor formation. Some people seem to find it difficult to obtain this chemical, though most chemists will obtain it if a kilogram is ordered. For these people it must be admitted that a flor can be obtained without gypsum, as our own experiments have proved, yet at the same time the sherry film flourishes much better on a wine where gypsum has been used than on an ordinary wine.

Alcohol also affects flor growth. It appears that sherry flor yeast can only live in certain alcoholic ranges. If a wine contains about 1.3 k (3 lb.) sugar per 4.5 litres (1 gal.), and this includes whatever sugar is in the fruit or vegetable used, one achieves the correct amount of alcohol, provided of course that fermentation is complete and almost all the sugar is converted into alcohol. For those who use a hydrometer the starting gravity range is from 110–120.

*In a Spanish bodega, a cellarman tests the clarity of Sherry by candlelight.*

Once the wine has finished fermenting it is racked into containers which are only three-quarters filled and the neck of the jar or bunghole is plugged with cotton wool, which is renewed occasionally. Then the wine must not be touched in any way until bottling time – no further racking, no movement, no disturbance of any kind.

**The Flor**

It is not difficult to recognise a flor. At first a few small islands of yeast appear. These gradually become more numerous until the whole surface is covered and the upper surface packs together until it seems like cheese with fine lines drawn across it. Underneath the yeast hangs down in short stringy lumps which eventually break off, fall to the bottom and autolyse, providing food for the surface yeast and also playing a big part in the ultimate flavour of the sherry.

If a flor is obtained, then the wine is best kept as a dry sherry. If on the other hand no flor is obtained, the sherry flavour will still appear to some extent (though not with so smooth a flavour) and the wine is best converted into a sweet sherry.

The following basic method is suitable for making all sherry type wines.

# Basic Method

1. Follow procedure detailed in the recipe for preparing the must and conducting the fermentation.

2. When fermentation is complete siphon off (rack) into a container big enough to allow a fair air space above the wine and plug with cotton wool. This racking is the only one in sherry making and it is all important that pulp debris does not get sucked into the new container. If by any chance this does occur it is best to do a second racking about two weeks later in order to remove this pulp.

3. Leave the jar in a cool place (12–15°C) and do not disturb.

4. A flor may form in a few weeks or months. The jar must then be left until all flor has finally sunk to the bottom, after which the wine can be bottled.

5. If a flor does not form (as should be the case for sweet oloroso type sherries) the wine can be sweetened with white grape

concentrate or sugar syrup shortly before bottling unless the wine-maker prefers to leave it dry. A raisin extract prepared by boiling 450 g (1 lb.) raisins in 1.1 litres (2 pt.) water for half an hour, carefully straining off pulp and evaporating the extract to about half its original volume, can also be used for sweetening.

# Original Dry Fino Sherry 1

(The recipe which demonstrated the possibility of flor formation in this country)

*Ingredients:*
    **450 g (1 lb.) bananas**
    **900 g (2 lb.) apples**
    **30 g (1 oz.) gypsum**
    **2 g (1/20 oz.) tannic acid**
    **4 g (1/7th oz.) ammonium phosphate (or 1 nutrient tablet)**
    **Sherry yeast**
    **560 g (1¼ lb.) sugar boiled up with 430 ml (¾ pt.) water and stored for use as detailed in the method**
    **Water to 4.5 litres (1 gal.)**
    **570 ml (1 pt.) white grape concentrate**
    **15 g (½ oz.) cream of tartar**
    **7½ g (¼ oz.) pectinol**

*Method:*
    Boil bananas, including skins, in 2 litres (4 pt.) of water for half an hour. Meanwhile core apples, chop and place in a polythene bucket. Strain liquor from bananas over apples. Add grape concentrate. Cover bucket with blanket and allow to cool. When cool add cream of tartar, gypsum, pectinol, tannic acid, ammonium phosphate and yeast starter. Stir twice daily, keeping well covered in between, and after three days strain off the apples and continue fermentation. Add the remaining sugar syrup from this point on at the rate of 150 ml (¼ pt.) per day until all has been absorbed, then top up with water to 4.5 litres (1 gal.). Thereafter continue from point 2 in basic method.

# Dry Fino Sherry 2

*Ingredients:*

450 g (1 lb.) parsnips
900 g (2 lb.) apples
450 g (1 lb.) sultanas
900 g (2 lb.) sugar dissolved
   in 570 ml (1 pt.) water
15 g (½ oz.) pectinol

Yeast nutrients
Sherry yeast starter
30 g (1 oz.) gypsum
15 g (½ oz.) tartaric acid
15 g (½ oz.) cream of tartar
Water to 4.5 litres (1 gal.)

*Method:*

   Scrub the parsnips and cut into chunks. Boil the latter in 3 litres (5 pt.) of water for 10 minutes, then strain off over raisins and sliced apple in a plastic bucket. Add all the other ingredients except the yeast, pectinol and 570 ml (1 pt.) of the sugar syrup (there should be 1.1 litres (2 pt.) altogether). When cool add the pectinol and the yeast starter and ferment on the pulp for four days, stirring twice daily. Keep the bucket well covered in the meantime to exclude insects. Strain off the pulp and add 150 ml (¼ pt.) of sugar syrup, and add the rest of the sugar syrup in 150 ml (¼ pt.) doses every three days. If a hydrometer is used add the sugar syrup whenever a gravity of five or less is recorded. Once the sugar additions are complete top up the jar to 4.5 litres (1 gal.) with water and thereafter proceed as detailed in the basic method.

# Dry Fino Sherry 3

*Ingredients:*

1.8 kg (4 lb.) greengages or yellow plums
450 g (1 lb.) peaches
225 g (½ lb.) sultanas or raisins
675 g (1½ lb.) sugar dissolved
430 ml (¾ pt.)
15 g (½ oz.) cream of tartar
Yeast nutrients
Sherry yeast starter
280 ml (½ pt.) white grape concentrate

30 g (1 oz.) gypsum
10 g (¼ oz.) pectinol
Water to 4.5 litres (1 gal.)

*Method:*

Wash and stone the greengages and peaches. Scald with 2 litres (4 pt.) boiling water in which the 15 g (½ oz.) cream of tartar has been dissolved. Add the sultanas or raisins, gypsum, yeast nutrient and 280 ml (½ pt.) of sugar syrup while the must is still hot. When cool add the pectinol and yeast starter and ferment on the pulp for two to three days. Strain off the pulp at the end of this time and add the grape concentrate. After seven days add 150 ml (¼ pt.) of sugar syrup and continue the addition of 150 ml (¼ pt.) of sugar syrup at 3-day intervals, until it has all been introduced. These sugar additions are best made every time the gravity of the must drops below five if a hydrometer is used. Finally top up to 4.5 litres (1 gal.) with water, and thereafter proceed as described in the basic method.

# Dry Fino Sherry 4
**(20 litres (4½ gal) cask maturing**

*Ingredients:*

| | |
|---|---|
| 6.5 kg (15 lb.) beetroot | 900 g (2 lb.) raisins |
| 1.8 kg (4 lb.) dried apricots | 30 g (1 oz.) pectinol |
| Sherry yeast starter | 110 g (4 oz.) gypsum |
| 2.25 litres (4 pt.) white grape conc. | 55 g (2 oz.) cream of tartar |
| 2.25 kg (5 lb.) sugar dissolved in | Water to 20 litres (4½ gal.) |
| 1.4 litres (2½ pt.) of water | Yeast nutrient |

*Method:*

Cut the beetroot into chunks and boil for half an hour in about 13 litres (3 gal.) of water. Strain liquor over washed apricots and raisins. Dissolve the cream of tartar while the must is still hot and add the gypsum, yeast nutrients and 570 ml (1 pt.) of sugar syrup. When cool add the pectinol and yeast starter and ferment on the pulp for 3–4 days. Strain off the pulp, press lightly and then add the grape concentrate. After 7–10 days add 570 ml (1 pt.) of sugar syrup and continue adding 570 ml (1 pt.) of sugar syrup every three days until it has all been introduced. The wine-maker using the hydrometer should follow the usual pattern of adding the pint of sugar syrup whenever a gravity of five or less is recorded. Finally top up to 20 litres (4½ gal.) with water and thereafter proceed as detailed in the basic method.

*Note* that this wine should be matured in cask for at least three years, otherwise it is apt to prove disappointing. Beetroot based wines are notoriously slow to develop but are capable of attaining excellent quality given sufficient time.

# Dry Fino Sherry 5

**(20 litres (4½ gal.) maturing)**

*Ingredients:*

| | |
|---|---|
| 1.8 kg (4 lb.) bananas | 45 g (1½ oz.) tartaric acid |
| 4 kg (9 lb.) parsnips | 30 g pectinol (1 oz.) |
| 900 g (2 lb.) raisins or sultanas | Yeast nutrients |
| 2.25 litres (4 pt.) white grape conc. | Sherry yeast starter |
| 55 g (2 oz.) cream of tartar | Sugar as required below |
| 110 g (4 oz.) gypsum | Water to 20 litres (4½ gal.) |

*Method:*

Scrub the parsnips and cut into chunks. Boil the latter in water for 10 minutes and carefully strain off the pulp. Peel the bananas, cut into slices and boil both skins and fruit in water for half an hour. Again carefully strain off the pulp. Boil the raisins or sultanas in water for half an hour, strain off the pulp carefully and boil the pulp with a fresh quantity of water for half an hour. Again strain off the pulp. Strain the combined banana, parsnip and raisin extracts again through a fine sieve or straining bag and dissolve the cream of tartar in the hot liquor. Also add the tartaric acid, yeast nutrients and gypsum at this stage, leaving the gypsum addition until last. Stir the must thoroughly to disperse the gypsum and ensure good mixing. When cool add the grape concentrate and sufficient sugar syrup and water to give 20 litres (4½ gal.) of must with an initial gravity of 110–120. Finally add the pectinol and yeast starter and ferment to dryness. Thereafter proceed as directed in the basic method. This wine should preferably be matured in cask and should be kept for several years before drinking, otherwise it is apt to be disappointing.

# Oloroso Sherry 1

**(20 litres (4½ gal.), cask maturing)**

*Ingredients:*
   **9 kg (20 lb.) apples**
   **4 kg ( 9 lb.) parsnips**
   **1.8 kg (4 lb.) figs**
   **1.8 kg (4 lb.) bananas**
   **3.6 kg (8 lb.) sugar dissolved in**
   **2.25 litres (4 pt.) water**
   **Water to 20 litres (4½ gal.)**
   **30 g (1 oz.) tartaric acid**
   **Yeast nutrients**
   **Sherry yeast starter**
   **2.25 litres (4 pt.) white grape concentrate**
   **30 g (1 oz.) pectinol**

*Method:*
   Scrub the parsnips and cut into chunks. Peel and slice the bananas, rejecting the skins. Boil the parsnips in water for 10 minutes, then strain off the pulp. Boil the banana slices in water for half-an-hour and again strain off the pulp. Wash the figs thoroughly and slice the apples. Pour the banana and parsnip extracts over the apples and figs and add the tartaric acid, yeast nutrients and 2.25 litres (4 pt.) of sugar syrup and adjust the volume to 15 litres (3–3½ gal.). When cool add the pectinol and yeast starter. Ferment on the pulp for 4–5 days, then strain off carefully and add the grape concentrate. After a further 10 days add 570 ml (1 pt.) of sugar syrup and repeat the addition every three days until all the syrup has been introduced (a hydrometer will considerably assist in judging the best time to add the sugar). Finally top up to 20 litres (4½ gal.) with water and thereafter proceed as specified in the basic method. Cask maturing for several years is advisable.

# Sweet Oloroso Sherry 2

*Ingredients:*

450 g (1 lb.) bananas
900 g (2 lb.) raisins
450 g (1 lb.) dried apricots
   or prunes (or 1.8 kg (4 lb.)
   fresh apricots)
10 g (¼ oz.) tartaric acid

Yeast nutrients
900 g (2 lb.) sugar dissolved in
   570 ml (1 pt.) water
10 g (¼ oz.) pectinol
Sherry yeast starter
Water to 4.5 litres (1 gal.)

*Method:*

Peel the bananas and cut into slices, rejecting the skins. Boil the slices in 3 litres (5 pt.) water for half an hour and strain over the other fruit (if fresh apricots are used these should be first stoned). Add the tartaric acid and yeast nutrients. When cool add the yeast and pectinol and ferment on the pulp for 3–4 days. Strain off the pulp at the end of this time and add 570 ml (1 pt.) sugar syrup. After 7–10 days add 150 ml (¼ pt.) sugar syrup and repeat the procedure every three days until all the sugar has been added. The hydrometer may be used to control the sugar additions in usual way. Finally top up to 4.5 litres (1 gal.) and thereafter proceed as in the basic method.

# Oloroso Sherry 3

*Ingredients:*

1.8 kg (4 lb.) parsnips
450 g (1 lb.) bananas
450 g (1 lb.) raisins
570 ml (1 pt.) white grape concentrate
15 g (½ oz.) tartaric acid
10 g (¼ oz. pectinol)
Yeast nutrients
Sherry yeast starter
675 g (1½ lb.) sugar dissolved in 430 ml (¾ pt.) water
Water to 4.5 litres (1 gal.)

*Method:*

Scrub the parsnips and cut into chunks. Peel the bananas and cut into slices. Boil both ingredients together or separately in a total of 2.25 litres (4 pt.) water and strain the hot liquor over the raisins. Add the yeast nutrient, tartaric acid and 280 ml (½ pt.) of sugar syrup. When cool add the pectinol and yeast starter. Ferment on the pulp for three days, then strain off the raisins and add the grape concentrate. After 7–10 days add 150 ml (¼ pt.) sugar syrup and add further doses of 150 ml (¼ pt.) at 3-day intervals until all the sugar has been added. Finally top up to 4.5 litres (1 gal.) with water and thereafter follow the instructions given in the basic method.

## Oloroso Sherry 4
**(Very full-bodied dessert)**

*Ingredients:*

| | |
|---|---|
| **900 g (2 lb.) bananas** | **10 g (¼ oz.) pectinol** |
| **900 g (2 lb.) peaches** | **Yeast nutrient** |
| **450 g (1 lb.) figs** | **675 g (1½ lb.) sugar dissolved** |
| **450 g (1 lb.) raisins** | **in 570 ml (1 pt.) water** |
| **570 ml (1 pt.) white grape conc.** | **Sherry yeast starter** |
| **Water to 4.5 litres (1 gal.)** | **15 g (½ oz.) tartaric acid** |

*Method:*

Peel and slice the bananas, rejecting the skins. Boil the slices in 2.25 litres (4 pt.) water for half an hour. Meanwhile wash figs and raisins thoroughly to remove dirt and possible sulphite; cut into halves. Strain the banana liquor over the figs raisins and stoned peaches. Add the tartaric acid, yeast nutrients and 280 ml (½ pt.) sugar syrup. When cool add the yeast and pectinol and ferment on the pulp for 2–3 days. Strain off the pulp carefully and add the grape concentrate. After 7–10 days add 150 ml (¼ pt.) sugar syrup and continue such additions at three day intervals until all the sugar has been introduced. The hydrometer may be used to control the sugar additions if desired. Finally top up to 4.5 litres (1 gal.) with water and thereafter proceed as detailed in the basic method.

# Full-Bodied Oloroso Sherry 5
(20 litres (4½ gal.) – cask maturing)

*Ingredients:*

9 kg (20 lb.) yellow plums or greengages
1.8 kg (4 lb.) dried apricots
2.7 kg (6 lb.) sugar dissolved in 1.7 litres (3 pt.) water
1.1 litres (2 pt.) white grape concentrate
30 g (1 oz.) pectinol
Yeast nutrients
1.8 kg (4 lb.) raisins
Sherry yeast starter
Water to 20 litres (4½ gal.)

*Method:*

Stone the plums or greengages and mix with the apricots and raisins. Scald with 13.5 litres (3 gal.) boiling water and add the yeast nutrients and 1.1 litres (2 pt.) sugar syrup. When cool add the pectinol and yeast starter and ferment on the pulp for four days. Strain off the pulp and press lightly and add the grape concentrate. After seven days add 150 ml (¼ pt.) repeat the additions every three days until all the sugar has been introduced. These sugar additions are of course best made with the aid of the hydrometer, Syrup being added at the rate of 150 ml (¼ pt.) per 4.5 litres (1 gal.) of must every time the gravity drops below five. Finally top up to 20 litres (4½ gal.) and thereafter proceed as in the basic method. This wine is best matured in cask for several years to allow its great potential to develop.

# CHAPTER III

# Port: Ever-popular

Of all the wines that amateur winemakers produce, a deep rich red wine is more often than not the favourite, and the remark is often heard regarding a choice home-made wine: "It's just like Port." In truth, many are not a bit like Port, but are just good dessert wines. Nevertheless, a careful analysis of their characteristics would show that had there been a few alterations to their ingredients or to their method of production, they could indeed have become very much like Port.

True ports, of course, are made from the grapes of the Douro Valley, in Portugal, and shipped to us from Oporto. Apart from white port, all ports are rich, red full-bodied wines, and these characteristics are the main points to have in mind when choosing the ingredients and their quantity. In addition, however, port has a distinctly fruity taste, which marks it off from many other dessert wines. In the commercial world this effect is achieved by stopping the fermentation with brandy before more than half the sugar in the must has been transformed into alcohol and carbon dioxide. Since few amateur winemakers will want to use this method, a careful choice of ingredients is needed to keep the fruity flavour. Another way is to mix a mature port-type wine with a younger one, and while the mature wine will impart its maturity to the younger one, the fruitiness of the young wine will tend to come through the blend. A happy evening can be spent tasting and comparing various blends in this way.

The high alcohol content of port (around 20%) is obtained by fortification, but because this is not envisaged in the ordinary way, very great care must be taken to start off with a well-balanced must rich in nutrients, and to ensure that sugar syrup is added little by little so that the very limit of alcohol production is reached.

*A port cellarman draws a sample.*

It is our impression that port yeasts do not reach as high an alcohol tolerance as some other yeasts, and this seems quite reasonable since in practice the yeast is never called upon to produce more than 5–10% alcohol before being killed off with brandy. If yeast manufacturers state that their port yeasts will in fact produce 18% alcohol under ideal conditions, then such yeasts are suitable for the purpose, but if in doubt it seems preferable to use a good Madeira yeast, which is certainly capable of this high figure. If Madeira wine were not heat-treated as part of its production, it would finish up very much more like port.

The two outstanding ingredients are undoubtedly elderberries and bilberries, though cherries and blackberries are also very suitable and sloes and damsons, raspberries, loganberries and blackcurrants are also very useful for imparting the fruitiness required. Red grape concentrate is also useful, though if used on its own it tends to produce a wine rather like British port-type wines, which are generally made in this manner. Its powerful function is to impart a vinous character to the wine.

The following recipes have been prepared on a graded basis of expense, ranging from inexpensive ones on the one hand where fruits are collected from the countryside, to one or two recipes of great magnificence on the other. These latter do produce wines of such richness, finesse and body that they compare favourably with most ports other than those of vintage or tawny quality. Their cost of making is often rather high by amateur winemaker standards. Still, it is worth making one such brew in a lifetime if only to reminisce about it in the evening of one's life.

In the recipes quantities of fresh fruit are quoted. Dried fruit such as elderberries and bilberries can always be substituted, 450 g (1 lb.) of these dried fruits being used in place of 1.3 kg (3 lb.) fresh elderberries or bilberries.

Similarly a packet of dried flowers can be used instead of fresh flowers (replacing 280 ml (½ pt.) of fresh flowers).

# Port – basic method

1. Prepare the must and commence the fermentation as directed in each recipe.

2. Add the sugar in stages as follows: If a hydrometer is employed add 150 ml (¼ pt.) sugar syrup per 4.5 litres (1 gal.) every

time the gravity drops to five or less. Continue these sugar additions until fermentation ceases. If no hydrometer is available the wine must be tasted regularly and the above 150 ml (¼ pt.) dose of sugar syrup per 4.5 litres (1 gal.) added whenever the wine tastes as if it contains little sugar. This latter procedure is of course much more hazardous and not really advisable in view of the easy control offered by the hydrometer. The sugar syrup is made by dissolving 900 g (2 lb.) sugar in 570 ml (1 pt.) water at the boil and allowing this solution to cool before use.

3. Rack the wine off its lees within a week of fermentation reaching completion. Add two Campden tablets per 4.5 litres (1 gal.).

4. Rack for a second time as soon as a significant new deposit forms or after three months, whichever is the sooner.

5. Carry out the third racking as per 4, above.

6. Rack at about four-monthly intervals after the third racking.

7. Persistent hazes should be removed by fining still present when the wine is one year old.

8. Store the wine for at least 12 months but preferably for 18-24 months. Casks are much better than glass for this purpose.

## RECIPE 1

*Ingredients:*

| | |
|---|---|
| **1.3 kg (3 lb.) elderberries** | |
| **900 g (2 lb.) bananas** | **Yeast nutrients** |
| **570 ml (1 pt.) red grape concentrate** | **Port yeast starter** |
| **225 g (½ lb.) raspberries** | **Sugar as required** |
| **280 ml (½ pt.) elderflowers** | **Water to 4.5 litres (1 gal.)** |

*Method:*

Peel the bananas (rejecting the skins) and cut into slices. Boil the latter in 2.25 litres (4 pt.) water for ½ hour, then strain carefully while still hot over the crushed elderberries and raspberries and add the yeast nutrients. When cool add the yeast starter and ferment on the pulp for not more than 24 hours. Strain off the pulp and press it lightly. Add the elderflowers and grape concentrate to the must and strain off the flowers three days later. Finally continue the fermentation as directed in the basic method.

(450 g (1 lb.) dried elderberries can be used here when fresh ones are not available).

## RECIPE 2

*Ingredients:*

2.7 kg (6 lb.) damsons
450 g (1 lb.) bananas
900 g (2 lb.) raisins
280 ml (½ pt.) elderflowers
10 g (¼ oz.) pectinol

Yeast nutrients
Port yeast starter
Sugar as required
Water to 4.5 litres (1 gal.)

*Method:*

Wash the raisins and damsons thoroughly and stone the latter. Peel the bananas (rejecting the skins) and cut into slices. Boil the banana slices in 3 litres (6 pt.) water for ½ hour, then strain while hot over the damsons and raisins. Add the yeast nutrients. When cool add the pectinol and yeast starter and ferment on the pulp for 3–4 days. Strain off the pulp and lightly press it. Add the elderflowers and strain off the flowers three days later. Thereafter proceed as directed in the basic method.

## RECIPE 3

*Ingredients:*

2.7 kg (6 lb.) cherries
450 g (1 lb.) bananas
570 ml (1 pt.) red grape conc.
225 g (½ lb.) raspberries
280 ml (½ pt.) elderflowers

Yeast nutrients
Port yeast starter
Sugar as required
Water to 4.5 litres (1 gal.)
10 g (¼ oz.) pectinol

*Method:*

Wash the cherries. Peel the bananas (rejecting the skins), cut into slices and boil in 2.25 litres (4 pt.) water for ½ hour. Strain while hot over the cherries and crushed raspberries and add the yeast nutrients. When cool add the pectinol, grape concentrate and yeast starter. Ferment on the pulp for 4–5 days, crushing the cherries daily to facilitate colour and juice extraction, then strain off carefully. Add the elderflowers and three days later strain off the flowers. Finally proceed as directed in the basic method.

## RECIPE 4

*Ingredients:*

1.3 kg (3 lb.) sloes
450 g (1 b.) bananas
450 g (1 lb.) raisins
570 ml (1 pt.) red grape conc.
280 ml (½ pt.) elderflowers

Yeast nutrients
Port yeast starter
Sugar as required
Water to 4.5 litres (1 gal.)
10 g (¼ oz.) pectinol

*Method:*

Peel the bananas (rejecting the skins), cut into slices and boil in 3 litres (5 pt.) water for ½ hour. Stone the sloes if possible but otherwise crush the fruit and strain the hot banana extract over the sloes and raisins. Add the yeast nutrients. When cool mix in the grape concentrate, pectinol and port yeast starter. Ferment on the pulp for two days then strain off and press lightly. Add the elderflowers and strain off again after three days. Thereafter continue as instructed in the basic method.


## RECIPE 5

*Ingredients:*

2.7 kg (6 lb.) bilberries
450 g (1 lb.) bananas
900 g (2 lb.) raisins
280 ml (½ pt.) elderflowers
Yeast nutrients

Port yeast starter
Sugar as required
Water to 4.5 litres (1 gal.)
10 g (¼ oz.) pectinol

*Method:*

Peel the bananas (rejecting the skins), cut into slices and boil in 3 litres (5 pt.) water for ½ hour. Strain while hot over the crushed bilberries and raisins. Add the yeast nutrients. When cool add the pectinol and yeast starter and ferment on the pulp for four days. Strain off the fruit, press lightly and add the elderflowers. Strain off the flowers after a further three days, then follow the instructions detailed in the basic method.

**RECIPE 6**

*Ingredients:*

1.8 kg (4 lb.) red plums
900 g (2 lb.) elderberries
570 ml (1 pt.) red grape conc.
280 ml (½ pt.) elderflowers
450 g (1 lb.) bananas

Yeast nutrients
Port yeast starter
Sugar as required
Water to 4.5 litres (1 gal.)
10 g (¼ oz.) pectinol

*Method:*

Peel the bananas (rejecting the skins), cut into slices and boil in 2.5 litres (4 pt.) water for ½ hour. Strain into a clean plastic bucket. Crush the elderberries and strain off the juice. Add 1.1 litres (2 pt.) hot banana extract to the residual elderberry pulp, stir and strain off again in five minutes. Repeat this leaching of the elderberry pulp with the remaining 1.1 litres (2 pt.) banana extract. Add the banana and elderberry extract to the washed stoned plums. Add the yeast nutrients. When cool (probably within a few hours in this case) add the pectinol and yeast starter. Ferment on the pulp for four days, then strain off carefully. Add the grape concentrate and elderflowers, straining off the latter after a further three days. Thereafter proceed as instructed in the basic method.

**RECIPE 7**

*Ingredients:*

1.3 kg (3 lb.) elderberries
1.3 kg (3 lb.) blackberries
450 g (1 lb.) raisins
570 ml (1 pt.) red grape conc.
450 g (1 lb.) bananas

280 ml (½ pt.) elderflowers
Yeast nutrients
Port yeast starter
Sugar as required
Water to 4.5 litres (1 gal.)

*Method:*

Peel the bananas (rejecting the skins), cut into slices and boil in 2.5 litres (4 pt.) water for ½ hour. Strain while hot over the crushed elderberries, blackberries and raisins and add the yeast nutrients. When cool, add the yeast starter and ferment on the pulp for 24 hours. Strain off and lightly press the pulp. Add the grape concentrate and elderflowers and strain off the latter three days later. Thereafter continue as instructed in the basic method.

## RECIPE 8

*Ingredients:*

2.7 kg (6 lb.) blackberries
450 g (1 lb.) bananas
900 g (2 lb.) raisins
280 ml (½ pt.) elderflowers

Yeast nutrients
Port yeast starter
Sugar as required
Water to 4.5 litres (1 gal.)

*Method:*

Peel the bananas (rejecting the skins), cut into slices and boil in 3 litres (6 pt.) water for ½ hour. Strain over the crushed blackberries and raisins and add the yeast nutrients. When cool add the yeast starter and ferment on the pulp for 2–3 days. Strain off and press the pulp lightly, then add the elderflowers. Strain off the flowers after a further three days. Finally proceed as directed in the basic method. This wine should go tawny within a few months. A 20 litre quantity of wine can be made by scaling up this recipe approximately so that the wine can then receive the benefits of cask maturing.

## RECIPE 9 (to make 20 litres (4½ gal.))

*Ingredients:*

6.5 kg (15 lb.) elderberries
3.1 kg (7 lb.) bananas
1.8 kg (4 lb.) raisins
1.1 litres (2 pt.) red grape conc.
1.1 litres (2 pt.) elderflowers

Yeast nutrients
Port yeast starter
Sugar as required
Water to 20 litres (4½ gal.)

*Method:* '

Peel the bananas (rejecting the skins), cut into slices and boil in about 12 litres (2½ gal.) water for ½ hour. Crush the elderberries and strain off the juice. Strain half of the hot banana extract over the elderberry pulp. Repeat the procedure with the remaining banana extract. Strain the banana and elderberry extracts again to remove as much pulp debris as possible, and the add the raisins and yeast nutrients. When cool add the elderflowers and yeast starter and ferment on the pulp for three days. Strain off the flowers and raisins, add the grape concentrate and thereafter continue as directed in the basic method. Cask maturing will benefit this wine considerably.

*Collecting winemaking ingredients, Portuguese style! The vintage is the season of comparative plenty for the peasants. Here, a whole village dances its way to work across the hills of the Alto Douro.*

**RECIPE 10 (to make 20 litres (4½ gal.))**

*Ingredients:*

5.5 kg (12 lb.) sloes
2.2 kg (5 lb.) elderberries
3.1 kg (7 lb.) bananas
2.25 litres (4 pt.) red grape conc.
1.1 litres (2 pt.) elderflowers

Yeast nutrients
Port yeast starter
Sugar as required
Water to 20 litres (4½ gal.)

*Method:*

Peel the bananas (rejecting the skins), cut into slices and boil in about 12 litres (2½ gal.) water for half an hour. Crush the elderberries and strain off the juice. Strain half the hot banana extract over the elderberry pulp, stir for five minutes and again strain off the pulp. Repeat this procedure with the remaining banana extract. Reject the elderberry pulp. Add the elderberry/banana extract to the crushed (preferably stoned) sloes and add the yeast nutrients. When cool add the yeast and ferment on the pulp for two days. Strain off and add the grape concentrate and elderflowers. After another three days strain off the flowers. Finally proceed as directed in the basic method. Cask maturing is again most advisable.

**RECIPE 11 (to make 20 litres (4½ gal.))**

*Ingredients:*

13 kg (30 lb.) cherries
3.1 kg (7 lb.) bananas
2.7 kg (6 lb.) raisins
1.3 kg (3 lb.) raspberries
1.1 litres (2 pt.) elderflowers

Yeast nutrients
Port yeast starter
Sugar as required
Water to 20 litres (4½ gal.)
15 g (½ oz.) pectinol

*Method:*

Peel the bananas (rejecting the skins), cut into slices and boil in about 12 litres (2½ gal.) water for ½ hour. Strain over the washed cherries and crushed raspberries and raisins and add the yeast nutrients. When cool add the pectinol and yeast starter. Ferment on the pulp for 4–5 days, crushing the cherries once or twice daily to break the skins and facilitate colour and juice extraction.

Strain off and lightly press the pulp. Add the elderflowers and strain off three days later. Thereafter continue as instructed in the basic method. Cask maturing is once more recommended for this wine.

**RECIPE 12 (to make 20 litres (4½ gal.))**

*Ingredients:*

5.4 kg (12 lb.) bilberries
5.4 kg (12 lb.) damsons
3.1 kg (7 lb.) bananas
1.8 kg (4 lb.) raisins
1.1 litres (2 pt.) red grape concentrate
1.1 litres (2 pt.) elderflowers
15 g (½ oz.) pectinol
Yeast nutrients
Port yeast starter
Sugar as required
Water to 20 litres (4½ gal.)

*Method:*

Peel the bananas (rejecting the skins), cut into slices and boil in about 12 litres (2½ gal.) for ½ hour. Strain over the crushed bilberries, stoned damsons and raisins and add the yeast nutrients. When cool add the pectinol and yeast starter and ferment on the pulp for three days. Strain off and lightly press the fruit. Add the grape concentrate and elderflowers and strain off in a further three days. Finally proceed as directed in the basic method. Cask maturing will improve this wine considerably.

# CHAPTER IV

# Hocks, Moselles and Alsatian Wines

There was once a Roman Emperor named Probus who became very worried about the idle temptations to which his troops fell victims along the Rhine boundary of the Roman Empire. The chroniclers were very discreet about the nature of the temptations involved, but it can be assumed that wine-drinking was not among them, since the solution arrived at by Probus was to employ the troops busily in planting the hillsides of the Rhine valley with grape-vines.

Out of this great endeavour has arisen through the centuries the superb group of white table wines known as Hocks and Moselles. The word superb is a relative description, since by no means all the wines of Germany (and Alsace) attain this high degree of excellence. Wines containing such appellations as Spatlese, Trockenbeeren-auslese, etc., are the product of vintage years when there is plenty of sunshine at the right time in this Northern outpost of viticulture. Some of these wines are very expensive and cost up to 12 guineas a bottle. Away down the scale are other wines which contain twice the amount of acid normally found in good amateur wines, and these are not always suitable to the British palate.

Moselles are very light dry wines, often drunk within a year of making, that have a charming delicate bouquet, are pleasing to the eye with their greenish tinge, and with their slatey fresh taste and low alcoholic strength are ideal thirst quenchers when served chilled on a hot summer's day.

48

*The unmistakable, graceful shape of the Hock or Moselle bottle.*

Hocks are fuller-bodied than Moselles, have more alcohol and flavour and when made from late-picked grapes are luscious enough to serve as a dessert wine.

The wines of Alsace rarely achieve the brilliance of Hocks and Moselles, but they are good honest dry white wines, about which it is said that "every sip becomes a swallow if you do not take care," and one can easily drink a bottle almost without noticing it – until one stands up to go home!

The type of yeast used is extremely important in making wines of any of these three types, but only certain of these yeasts are available to amateur winemakers. The following table outlines those available at the moment, and summarises the type of wine to which each yeast corresponds:

| Moselle Wines | Approx. Alcoholic strength | Character of the Wine |
|---|---|---|
| Zeltinger | 7–9% | Very light, dry and fairly acid. Slightly sweeter and fuller-bodied |
| *Bernkastler | | in very good years, e.g. 1959. |
| *Hocks* Niersteiner | 9%–12% | Medium to fairly fullbodied. Fairly |
| *Steinberg | | dry, ranging through medium-dry |
| Rudesheim | | to medium in sweetness. Can be |
| *Johannisberger | | fairly acid, especially in poorer |
| Liebfraumilch | | years. |
| *Alsatian Wines* Riesling | 10%–12% | Fairly light and slightly acid. Fairly |
| Sylvaner | | dry but ranging to medium-dry or |
| Traminer | | medium in sweetness. |
| Gewurztraminer | | |

*Those types marked with an asterisk are generally recognised as attaining very good quality and rank among the best German wines. Steinberg yeast is one of the most reliable types currently available to amateur winemakers.

In preparing a gospel of perfection, we have suggested the very best strains. If at anytime you find them unobtainable settle for a Hock yeast or a general purpose white yeast.

It is seen that the alcoholic strength is little more than that of double-strength beers, and indeed many of the lighter wines are gulped rather than sipped. It is difficult for many amateur wine-makers to restrain themselves from building up the alcohol by adding more and more sugar syrup to the fermenting must, but it must be emphasised that these wines are very light in body and alcohol, and they will lose their character if they are made into strongly alcoholic types.

Since the yeast plays so important a part in the flavouring of the ultimate wine, it is important not to extract too much flavour from the ingredients, and lengthy pulp fermentation is to be avoided.

We must also emphasise here a matter which is important to all white ·wine production, and that is the danger of oxidation. If white wines are exposed to too much air at racking time, or if they are matured in small casks, they develop a bouquet somewhat like a sherry bouquet, except that the wine does not taste like sherry. This "maderisation," as it is called, constitutes a spoilt wine. It is extremely common in amateur winemaking circles, and the only way to avoid this danger is to ensure that every racking is carried out as quickly as possible without much splashing that forces carbon dioxide out of solution and admits air to the wine, and that sulphiting is carried out immediately after each racking at 100 parts per million (two Campden tablets per 4.5 litres (1 gal.)). If it is intended to mature white wine in casks smaller than 40 litres (9 gal.), it is best to varnish the two end panels to cut down the amount of air entering the wine through the pores of the wood.

One additional point requires close attention in the production of these wine types, is the need to have a long cool fermentation. These wines do not have the robust flavour of elderberry or parsnip or raspberry. They are delicate, and the flavours released by the yeast must not be dissipated into the air by a vigorous fermen-tation. Consequently a fermenting temperature of 15–17°C (60–65°F) is better (or even 13–15°C 55–60°F), even though this may mean a longer fermentation.

Before detailing the basic method and recipes, let us say a word about serving these wines. Some people drink them out of hock glasses fairly well chilled. They also have a purpose as a long thirst-quenching drink in summer when served as two-thirds wine, one third soda-water and a few ice cubes in half pint tumblers.

With a slice of lemon on top it is a very attractive drink for a hot summer's day.

**Basic Procedure**

1. Process fruit, etc., and commence fermentation as outlined under each individual recipe.

2. When fermentation is *almost* complete (gravity down to 1.000) rack carefully without splashing into fresh jars, and sulphite 100 p.p.m. – two Campden tablets per 4.5 litres (1 gal.). It is very important not to carry over any fruit pulp at this racking and if by any chance this does occur, it will tend to sink to the bottom of the jar in about 10 days, whereupon the wine should be racked again carefully and a further one Campden tablet per 4.5 litres (1 gal.) added (50 p.p.m.). This sulphite will have disappeared by the time of the next racking.

3. A light yeast sediment should form, and the wine can be safely left on this for four months, after which the wine should again be racked and once more sulphited at two Campden tablets per 4.5 litres (1 gal.) (100 p.p.m.).

4. The wine should then be bottled immediately after this racking and sulphiting and a further few months in bottle will mature it. These wines improve up to 2–3 years, but after that will not normally attain further improvement unless of exceptional merit.

**RECIPE 1 (Hock)**

*Ingredients:*

1.8 kg (4 lb.) rhubarb
450 g (1 lb.) raisins          675 g (1½ lb). honey (or
280 ml (½ pt.) white grape conc.          450 g (1 lb.) sugar)
280 ml (½ pt.) elderflowers          Steinberg yeast starter
Nutrients          Water to 4.5 litres (1 gal.)

*Method:*

Wash the rhubarb and cut into chunks. Press the chunks and strain the juice carefully to remove suspended pulp debris. If no press is available, the chunks may be crushed, the juice strained off and the pulp extracted twice with 1.1 litres (2 pt.) *cold* water each time. The combined extracts should then be strained carefully. Add sufficient water to make up the volume of 3 litres

52

(6 pt.), then add the nutrients, washed raisins, elderflowers and yeast starter. Ferment on the pulp for 2–3 days, then strain off and press the pulp lightly. Add the grape concentrate and honey (dissolved in 570 ml (1 pt.) water) and make up the volume to 4.5 litres (1 gal.). Thereafter proceed as directed in the basic procedure.

*NOTE:*
Chalk treatment should not be attempted here. The above procedure, especially pressing, prevents an unduly large amount of oxalic acid from entering the must. Hot extraction procedures must be avoided for this reason.

**RECIPE 2 (Hock)**
*Ingredients:*
   **450 g (1 lb) raisins**
   **570 ml (1 pt.) white grape concentrate**
   **430 ml (¾ pt.) elderflowers**
   **675 g (1½ lb.) honey (or 450 g (1 lb.) sugar)**
   **Nutrients**
   **Rudesheim Yeast Starter**
   **Water to 4.5 litres (1 gal.)**
   **15 g (½ oz.) malic acid**

*Method:*
Wash the raisins and add to 3 litres (6 pt.) water. Add the elderflowers, grape concentrate, malic acid and nutrients and stir thoroughly to mix the ingredients. Add the yeast starter and ferment on the pulp for 2–3 days. Strain off the pulp and press lightly. Add the honey (dissolved in 570 ml (1 pt.) water) and sufficient water to make up the volume to 4.5 litres (1 gal.). Thereafter continue as instructed in the basic procedure.

**RECIPE 3 (Moselle)**
*Ingredients:*

| | |
|---|---|
| **1.8 kg (4 lb.) green gooseberries** | **15 g (½ oz.) pectinol** |
| **570 ml (1 pt.) white grape conc.** | **Nutrients** |
| **430 ml (¾ pt.) elderflowers** | **Zeltinger yeast starter** |
| **450 g (1 lb.) honey** | **Water to 4.5 litres (1 gal.)** |

*Method:*

Top and tail and wash the gooseberries. Scald with 3 litres (6 pt.) boiling water and add the honey and nutrients. When cool crush the fruit by hand then add the elderflowers, pectinol and yeast starter. Ferment on the pulp for two days, then strain off and press the pulp lightly. Add the grape concentrate and sufficient water to make the volume up to 4.5 litres (1 gal.). Thereafter proceed as instructed in the basic procedure.

**RECIPE 4 (Liebfraumilch)**

*Ingredients:*

**1.8 kg (4 lb.) cooking apples (Bramleys)**
**900 g (2 lb.) dessert apples**
**450 g (1 lb.) raisins**
**280 ml (½ pt.) white grape concentrate**
**280 ml (½ pt.) elderflowers**
**450 g (1 lb.) sugar (or 675 g (1½ lb.) honey)**
**Nutrients**
**Liebfraumilch yeast starter**
**Water to 4.5 litres (1 gal.)**

*Method:*

Wash the apples, cut into slices and press out the juice. Strain out suspended pulp particles carefully. Add sufficient water to bring the volume up to 3 litres (6 pt.), then add the sugar (dissolved in 280 ml (½ pt.) water), nutrients, raisins, elderflowers and yeast starter. Ferment on the pulp for 2–3 days, then strain off the pulp and press lightly. Add the grape concentrate and sufficient water to make the volume up to 4.5 litres (1 gal.). Thereafter continue as directed in the basic procedure.

If no press is available, the apple slices may be scalded with 2.25 litres (4 pt.) boiling water, the nutrients, raisins and sugar added. Add the elderflowers and yeast starter when cool and subsequently proceed as above. This method is less satisfactory than that described above, though still worth trying. It is advisable to add 15 g (½ oz.) pectinol with the elderflowers when employing this method.

**RECIPE 5 (Moselle)**

*Ingredients:*

1.7 litres (3 pt.) dandelion petals
570 ml (1 pt.) white grape concentrate
675 g (1½ lb.) honey                   **Nutrients**
20 g (⅔ oz.) malic acid                **Bernkastler yeast starter**
10 g (⅓ oz.) tartaric acid             **Water to 4.5 litres (1 gal.)**

*Method:*

Scald the dandelion petals and honey with 3 litres (6 pt.) boiling water. Add the nutrients, malic and tartaric acids. When cool add the yeast starter. Ferment on the pulp for two days, then strain off and press the pulp lightly. Add the grape concentrate and sufficient water to bring the volume up to 4.5 litres (1 gal.). Thereafter proceed as directed in the basic procedure.

*NOTE:*

The dandelions should be gathered on a dry sunny day, otherwise contamination with insects and undesirable micro-organisms may be encountered. The petals are best separated from the head with scissors – it is a very laborious task by hand!


**RECIPE 6 (Hock)**

*Ingredients:*

1.8 kg (4 lb.) peaches
450 g (1 lb.) raisins
280 ml (½ pt.) white grape concentrate
280 ml (½ pt.) rose petals
450 g (1 lb.) honey (or 335 g (¾ lb.) sugar)
**Nutrients**
15 g (½ oz.) pectinol
**Johannisberger yeast starter**
**Water to 4.5 litres (1 gal.)**

*Method:*

Stone the peaches and press out the juice. Strain out pulp debris carefully. Dilute to 3 litres (6 pt.) with water and add the nutrients, washed raisins, honey (dissolved in 280 ml (½ pt.) water) and pectinol. Finally add the yeast starter and rose petals and ferment on the pulp for two days. Strain off the pulp and press lightly. Add the grape concentrate and sufficient water to make the volume up to 4.5 litres (1 gal.). Thereafter proceed as directed in the basic procedure but rack for the first time at a gravity of 5–10.

*NOTE:*

Pulp fermentation of the peaches is permissible though pressing is preferable. Add the stoned peaches to 2.25 litres (4 pt.) water together with the raisins, etc., and then pulp ferment for two days exactly as recommended above.

It is also important to note that delicately perfumed rose petals should be used. With strongly scented petals 150 ml (¼ pt.) per 4.5 litres (1 gal.) will suffice.

**RECIPE 7 (Hock)**

*Ingredients:*

675 g (1½ lb.) gooseberries
225 g (½ lb.) raisins
570 ml (1 pt.) white grape concentrate
20 g (⅔ oz.) malic acid
450 g (1 lb.) honey (or 335 g (¾ lb.) sugar)
Nutrients
Niersteiner yeast starter
Water to 4.5 litres (1 gal.)

*Method:*

Scald the crushed gooseberries and raisins with 3 litres (6 pt.) boiling water. Add the nutrients, honey and malic acid. When cool add the yeast starter. Ferment on the pulp for 1–2 days, then strain off and press the pulp lightly. Add the grape concentrate and sufficient water to bring the volume up to 4.5 litres (1 gal.). Thereafter proceed as instructed in the basic procedure.

## RECIPE 8 (Hock)

*Ingredients:*

450 g (1 lb.) white currants
1.1 litres (2 pt.) orange juice
570 ml (1 pt.) white grape concentrate
675 g (1½ lb.) honey
Nutrients
Steinberg yeast starter
Water to 4.5 litres (1 gal.)

*Method:*

Juice sufficient oranges to provide 1.1 litres (2 pt.) juice. Strain the latter carefully to remove suspended pulp particles and add to the crushed white currants. Add 2.25 litres (4 pt.) water, the nutrients and honey (dissolved in 430 ml (¾ pt.) water). Add the yeast starter and ferment on the pulp for two days. Strain off the pulp and press lightly. Add the grape concentrate and sufficient water to bring the volume up to 4.5 litres (1 gal.). Thereafter proceed as directed in the basic procedure, racking for the first time at a gravity of five.


## RECIPE 9
### Hock, 20 litres (4½ gal.) . Short cask maturing (3–6 months)

*Ingredients:*

7.8 kg (18 lb.) rhubarb
2.25 litres (4 pt.) white grape concentrate
1.1 litres (2 pt.) rose petals
2.25 kg (5 lb.) honey
Nutrients
Steinberg yeast starter
Water to 20 litres (4½ gal.)

*Method:*

Wash the rhubarb and cut into chunks. Press the chunks and strain the juice carefully to remove suspended pulp particles. If no press is available the rhubarb may be crushed and the juice strained off. The pulp may then be extracted twice with 6.75 litres

57

(1½ gal.) cold water each time and the combined juice and extracts strained carefully as above. Add the grape concentrate, nutrients, honey (dissolved in 2.75 litres (5 pt.) water) and rose petals. Make up the volume to 20 litres (4½ gal.) and ferment on the pulp for two days. Strain off the pulp and make up the volume to 20 litres (4½ gal.) with water. Thereafter proceed as directed in the basic procedure, but rack for the first time at a gravity of about 8.

*NOTE:*

The rhubarb juice should not be treated with chalk for the reasons mentioned in an earlier recipe.


**RECIPE 10**
**(Alsatian, 20 litres (4½ gal.) . Cask maturing for three months)**
*Ingredients:*

7.8 kg (18 lb.) green gooseberries
1.8 kg (4 lb.) raisins
1.1 litres (2 pt.) white grape concentrate
1.7 litres (3 pt.) elderflower
30 g (1 oz.) pectinol
1.8 kg (4 lb.) sugar
Nutrients
Traminer yeast starter
Water to 20 litres (4½ gal.)


*Method:*

Wash the gooseberries and raisins and scald with 13.5 litres (3 gal.) boiling water. Add the nutrients and sugar and stir until dissolved. When cool crush the fruit by hand, then add the pectinol, elderflower and yeast starter. Ferment on the pulp for two days, then strain off and press the pulp lightly. Add the grape concentrate and make the volume up to 20 litres (4½ gal.) with water. Thereafter continue as instructed in the basic procedure.

# CHAPTER V

# Dry Red Wines of France

The varieties of dry red wines are so numerous that only a general classification is possible.

From the great vintages of Bordeaux (Claret) and the mighty Burgundies to wines from remote villages in South America, red wine is perhaps the most widely consumed wine in the world, the mainstay of those areas where water is used only for washing.

It might be as well to mention Algerian wines first, since their production totals many million gallons each year. These wines are commonly used for blending with the mediocre and nameless wines of Bordeaux, Burgundy and, specially, the Midi to provide the vin ordinaire which is the staple wine of the French working classes. Very little of the blended wine is exported, but enormous quantities are consumed in France – it is the "bread-and-butter" wine of the shippers.

Some cheap Algerian wine is also used by less scrupulous shippers to stretch the better but less plentiful Burgundies and thereby increase profits. This is a highly reprehensible practice possible with Burgundies because the many small vineyards sell their wines directly to the shippers for blending with other wines from the district. It is then all too easy to slip in a little Algerian wine. Claret is rarely adulterated in this way as the vineyard holdings are much larger and the good quality wines are rarely blended. The climate in Algeria is such that the vine grows well and crops are enormous so that in consequence quality tends to suffer.

**Many of the better amateur red wines taste rather like Algerian wine, and this is no stigma, for it is an achievement to produce a dry red wine from ingredients such as elderberries and raisins which tastes like a grape wine – an achievement not reached in "grandmother's day" whatever the traditionalists might say.**

*In a small square under the shadow of Sacré Coeur Church in Montmartre a connoisseur in the finery of a "militiaman of the republic of Montmartre" samples a new Bordeaux "clairet" – the "claret" beloved of Britons.*

Beaujolais is the second wine that commands our attention, for we have found by experiment and from judging that when an amateur winemaker produces a really outstanding dry red wine it seems to be more often like a Beaujolais than any other dry red wine. Beaujolais can be bought by the glass in most pubs, and it is worth trying a few glasses to get the taste of it before trying to produce a wine of this type. Beaujolais comes from the most southerly and largest of the Burgundy wine producing areas, and it is a good average-quality light red wine that matures early. The Burgundians have a vast rivalry with their Claret-producing neighbours in Bordeaux, and they say in their confident superiority that Burgundy does NOT leave your mouth feeling like the bottom of a parrot's cage, a scornful reference to the practice in Bordeaux of putting young wines in new oak casks which causes additional tannin to be released into the wine from the oak. They also have a saying in the Beaujolais region that every sip becomes a swallow and every swallow a guzzle, after which presumably you lay in the sun and sleep it off. Undoubtedly Beaujolais has become a very popular wine in this country, and it is perhaps the easiest of the dry red wines to simulate, often being ready to drink at 1–2 years.

## Tiny Vineyards

The great majority of truc Burgundies other than Beaujolais come from the Cote de Nuits and Cote de Beaune. One thing which should warm the hearts of amateur winemakers to this region of France is the fact that the whole area is split up into tiny vineyards, so that there are over 20,000 vineyard owners. Most of these work at other jobs during the week, tending their minute vineyards in the evenings and at week-ends, rather as the English do their allotments. The annual production of wine from one of these vineyards is often less than that of the larger amateur winemakers of this country. The owners may in many ways be regarded as amateur winemakers at heart, who make wine for the sheer love of it and just happen to sell part of their production by chance, as it were, the tiny parcels of wine being handled by co-operatives.

**Unfair introduction**

Let us now take a closer look at Bordeaux where the red wines known collectively as Claret are produced. Bordeaux can well afford to shrug off its disclaimers, for the leading connoisseurs over many centuries have affirmed, and no doubt will for centuries to come, that Claret is the absolute monarch of all dry red wines. Even Burgundy pales beside it provided one has drunk enough to obtain a palate. It is an unfortunate occurrence in this country that more often than not one's first encounter with Claret is at a firm's annual dinner, where, after having had a few gins or whiskies at the reception before the dinner, everyone moves into the dining hall and comes face to face with claret, served with the meal, generally an inferior claret. Under these conditions, the claret tastes like vinegar and one forms the impression that claret is not a wine with which to make closer acquaintance.

For those who have suffered this fate, and their number is surprisingly high, it is better to drink Burgundy, and if you drink enough you will in time graduate to Claret as naturally as Summer follows Spring. One's palate becomes steadily drier the more wine one drinks, and clarets are on the whole drier than Burgundy, while possessing in addition a greater finesse that only earnest drinking will make apparent.

The best Clarets are those which at the outset contain too much tannin (like an elderberry wine made with 2.7 kg (6 lb.) berries to 4.5 litres (1 gal.)). At one year old such a wine is harsh and almost undrinkable, but since Clarets are kept maturing in cask for 2–3 years (and sometimes up to 5 years) and in bottle for another 2–20 years, they assume a quality at the end of this time not possible to less tannic wines which mature earlier.

Claret is then the absolute goal towards which the amateur winemaker strives in his winemaking, since Claret is the best of the dry red wines, and dry red wines are the hardest types of wine to produce successfully. To achieve this goal is difficult, but it can in fact be done. The secret is first to obtain a well-balanced must and secondly to allow proper maturing, if possible in a cask.

In order to approach the desired goal, the must has to conform to certain basic essentials, i.e.:–

1. A deep red fruit must be used, and for this purpose elderberries, bilberries, deep red plums, damsons, cherries, sloes, choke-

cherries are suitable whereas blackberries are not, since their colour fades with time.

2. A second ingredient is required to provide vinous quality. This can be red grape concentrate, raisins or sultanas. It is not advisable to try to make good dry red wines from red grape concentrate alone since the resultant wine appears to lack character.

3. The must should be rich in tannin, richer for Claret than Burgundy type wines, so that the wine will prove too harsh for drinking at 6 months.

4. An average acidity of 3.3–4.3 p.p.t. (in terms of sulphuric acid) is desirable with 3.8 p.p.t. offering a good average value.

5. It should have an alcoholic content of 10–13% approx. (equivalent to a starting gravity of 75–100).

6. A good red wine yeast should be used such as Pommard, Burgundy or Bordeaux.

In the following recipes, these factors have been taken care of automatically, and it is only necessary to point out that one cannot be sure whether one's intended Claret turns out more like a Beaujolais or vice versa, so that if one is going to name one's wine in this fashion it is better to wait until bottling time before christening it. Where we have indicated a recipe as a Claret (Recipes 3 and 6), its tannin content is higher than that of Burgundy recipes so that adequate maturing will be needed. If the winemaker cannot afford to wait two years for maturing it is better to stick to the Burgundy and Beaujolais recipes.

**Basic Procedure**

It should be noted that all recipes are quoted for 20 litre (4½ gal.) quantities. This is a normal cask size used by amateur winemakers in Britain, and is really the minimum size capable of producing top-quality dry red wines. The quantities of ingredients can of course be scaled up or down for larger or smaller volumes of wine. The main essential is that cask maturing should be practised with red wines where possible.

1. Proceed as per recipe in processing ingredients and commencing fermentation.

2. When fermentation has proceeded to dryness rack carefully into a fresh container. This first racking may be into a polypin, where it can easily be discerned, after a week or so, whether the wine is clear of pulp debris. If any large amount of such deposit is apparent, rack once more into a cask, this time sulphiting with 50 p.p.m. (1 Campden tablet per 4.5 litres (1 gal.)).

3. Successive rackings should be made at 4-month intervals for at least 1 year, and preferably 2 years. At each racking the wine should be tasted. During the early rackings, it should appear rather harsh, undrinkable but with a certain vinous character. Gradually it should be possible to perceive an element of smoothness creeping in and a disappearance of the harsh initial character.

4. When the wine appears almost drinkable, it should be bottled and the bottles stored for a further 6 months at least.

5. If one intends to enter these wines in competitions it is worth-while bottling part of the wine in screw-top quart beer or cider bottles. In this way, any deposit or crust which may form, quite common with red wines, will settle at the bottom and an ordinary wine-bottle can be filled from the beer bottle without this sediment being siphoned over with the wine.


## RECIPE 1

*Ingredients:*

| | |
|---|---|
| **4.5 kg (10 lb.) elderberries** | **Nutrients** |
| **4.5 kg (10 lb.) raisins** | **Beaujolais yeast starter** |
| **1.8 kg (4 lb.) sugar** | **Water to 20 litres (4½ gal.)** |

*Method:*

Crush the elderberries and strain off the juice. Leach the pulp by adding 4.5 litres (1 gal.) of boiling water, stirring for 5 minutes and then straining off the pulp. Repeat this treatment with a second 4.5 litres (1 gal.) of boiling water. Add the raisins and nutrients to this elderberry extract followed by another 6 litres (1½ gal.) water. When cool add the yeast starter and ferment on the raisin pulp for 4 days. Strain off the pulp and press lightly. Add the sugar, stir until completely dissolved and make up the volume to 20 litres (4½ gal.) with water. Thereafter continue as directed in the basic procedure.

## RECIPE 2

*Ingredients:*

9 kg (20 lb.) cherries
1.8 kg (4 lb.) raisins        Nutrients
1.1 litres (2 pt.) red grape conc.   Pommard yeast starter
1.8 kg (4 lb.) sugar         Water 20 litres (4½ gal.)

*Method:*

Add 15 litres (3½ gal.) boiling water to the washed cherries and raisins. Add the nutrients and sugar and stir until dissolved. When cool add the yeast starter. Ferment on the pulp until a sample drawn off from the bulk is sufficiently deep in colour. Strain off and press the pulp lightly. Add the grape concentrate and make the volume up to 20 litres (4½ gal.) with water. Thereafter proceed as instructed in the basic procedure.

## RECIPE 3 (Claret)

*Ingredients:*

5.4 kg (12 lb.) elderberries
2.2 kg (5 lb.) greengages
1.1 litres (2 pt.) red grape concentrate
2.7 kg (6 lb.) sugar
Nutrients
Bordeaux yeast starter
Water to 20 litres (4½ gal.)

*Method:*

Crush the elderberries and strain off the juice. Leach the pulp by adding 4.5 litres (1 gal.) boiling water, stirring for 5 minutes, then straining off the pulp. Repeat this procedure with a second 4.5 litres (1 gal.) of boiling water. Add the stoned greengages, sugar, nutrients and 4.5 litres (1 gal.) of water to this elderberry extract and stir well until dissolved. When cool add the yeast starter. Ferment on the pulp for 4 days then strain off the pulp and press lightly. Add the grape concentrate and make the volume up to 20 litres (4½ gal.) with water. Thereafter proceed as instructed in the basic procedure.

# RECIPE 4

*Ingredients:*

5.4 kg (12 lb.) bilberries
4.5 kg (10 lb.) peaches      **Nutrients**
1.1 litres (2 pt.) red grape conc.      **Burgundy yeast starter**
2.7 kg (6 lb.) sugar      **Water to 20 litres (4½ gal.)**

## Method

Crush the bilberries and add the stoned peaches. Add 10 litres (2½ gal.) boiling water, sugar and nutrients and stir until disolved. When cool add the yeast starter. Ferment on the pulp until a satisfactory depth of colour is attained then strain off the pulp and press lightly. Add the grape concentrate and sufficient water to make the volume up to 20 litres (4½ gal.). Thereafter proceed as instructed in the basic procedure.

# RECIPE 5

*Ingredients:*

11 kg (25 lbs.) dessert apples
5.4 kg (12 lb.) elderberries
1.1 litres (2 pt.) red grape concentrate
2.25 kg (5 lb.) sugar
**Nutrients**
**Pommard yeast starter**
**Water to 20 litres (4½ gal.)**

## Method:

Crush the elderberries and strain off the juice. Add 4.5 litres (1 gal.) boiling water to the pulp, stir for 5 minutes then strain off the pulp. Repeat this treatment with a further 4.5 litres (1 gal.) of boiling water. Add the elderberry juice and hot extracts to the washed sliced apples. Dissolve the sugar and nutrients in this solution. When cool add the yeast starter. Ferment on the pulp for 7 days then strain off the pulp and press lightly. Add the grape concentrate and sufficient water to make the volume up to 20 litres (4½ gal.). Thereafter proceed as directed in the basic procedure.

### RECIPE 6 (Claret)

*Ingredients:*

**5.4 kg (12 lb.) sloes or damsons**
**1.8 kg (4 lb.) raisins**
**2.25 litres (4 pt.) red grape concentrate**
**1.8 kg (4 lb.) honey**
**Nutrients**
**Bordeaux yeast starter**
**Water to 20 litres (4½ gal.)**

*Method:*

Wash and crush the sloes and mix with the raisins. (Stone the sloes if possible). Add the honey, nutrients and 12 litres (3 gal.) of boiling water. When cool add the yeast starter and ferment on the pulp for 2–3 days. Strain off the pulp and press lightly. Add the grape concentrate and sufficient water to bring the volume up to 20 litres (4½ gal.). Thereafter continue as instructed in the basic procedure. This wine will require fairly long maturing and is best not attempted unless cask maturing is contemplated.

### RECIPE 7

*Ingredients:*

**11 kg (25 lb.) plums (red or blue)**
**1.8 kg (4 lb.) raisins**
**2.25 litres (4 pt.) red grape concentrate**
**900 g (2 lb.) honey**
**Nutrients**
**Pommard yeast starter**
**Water to 20 litres (4½ gal.)**
**30 g (1 oz.) pectinol**

*Method:*

Wash and stone the plums and add the raisins and honey. Add 12 litres (3 gal.) boiling water and the nutrients. When cool add the pectinol and yeast starter. Ferment on the pulp for 5–6 days then strain off the pulp and press lightly. Add the red grape concentrate and sufficient water to make the volume up to 20 litres (4½ gal.). Thereafter proceed as directed in the basic procedure.

# CHAPTER VI

# White Wines of France

During one of the many wars that England has waged against France, an English general is purported to have said that he found the greatest difficulty in working up the proper feeling of hostility, since whenever he thought of wine he immediately thought of France, and whenever he thought of France he remembered her rich vineyards. To destroy those vineyards was to him a monstrous sin.

Doubtless the general was replaced by another who preferred Port, but the vineyards remain, despite wars and other calamities, and from their verdant richness pours forth each year a refreshing river of wine greater in volume than that of any other country in the world.

**A great deal of this wine is red, of course, but of the many white wines produced, there are three main types which merit closer attention, and which can be simulated by the amateur winemaker once he has realised the basic characteristics of each type.**

These three main types are **White Burgundy, Graves** and **Sauternes.** It should be mentioned, however, that there are many other excellent white wine producing areas of France which we have omitted solely because they are as yet not sufficiently well-known in this country. **White Burgundies** are made from grapes that are fully but not over-ripened. Since all the sugar is converted to alcohol during fermentation, a dry, full-bodied, velvety wine results.

The great name in white Burgundies is **Montrachet,** a name familiar to anyone who has travelled to the Riviera down the famous Route Nationale 6 as it passes through part of the Cote d'Or near Chagny. Many wines from adjacent vineyards in the same area trade on the fame of Montrachet by attaching its name to their own, e.g. Puligny-Montrachet. These are all fine wines, but the very best, labelled simply Le Montrachet, is so rare that barely a thousand bottles of wine reach the whole of Britain each year (at £9.00 a bottle).

**Pouilly-Fuisse** is also well-known, and is frequently served chilled with sea-food. At its best it is a superb but short-lived wine, which often figures in off-licence "Sale Price" offers after it is five years old, a good indication of its approaching senility.

**Chablis** is perhaps the best known of white Burgundies. Chablis have a certain crispness with a slight acidity, the colour is golden with a tinge of green, and all have a sort of gunmetal aftertaste arising from the flinty soil that distinguishes them from other white wines.

Since comparatively little white Burgundy is usually produced its price is often high in comparison with other white wines. One cheap white Burgundy can be found, however, and this is **Macon Blanc.**

An interesting fact emerges here. In our search for ingredients that will make satisfactory substitutes for the grape, the obvious sometimes escapes us. In one issue of the "Amateur Winemaker" there was an article on the use of Apricot pulp as one of the best ingredients for a beginner. We were drinking some eight-month-old wine (made according to the recommended recipe) in the office one day recently, when someone said "Let's go round to the 'Golden Eagle' for a drink." (One might consider this a super-fluous remark, but never mind!). While the ladies of the office went over to gin and bitter lemon, one of the authors asked for white wine and was given the Macon Blanc. It was astonishing to find that the Apricot and the Macon Blanc were identical in flavour and the Macon only scored in the matter of bouquet, a fact that could easily be remedied by the inclusion of flowers, e.g. elder-flowers. It is worth trying that recipe, for Macon Blanc is one of the best **cheap** white wines that is drunk.

Fruits such as green gooseberries, apricots or oranges are emi-nently suitable for producing Chablis type wines, but generally some white grape concentrate or sultanas are needed in addition in order to obtain the true vinosity. A good Chablis yeast is required, and to obtain the best results from this yeast, great care must be taken both to avoid long pulp fermentations and to pre-

*Bottling sessions are the same everywhere!*

serve the delicate flavour by careful racking. All too many wine-makers rack their wines with a great deal of splashing, which forces bouquet out of the wine, and/or causes too much oxidisation, and insist on obtaining the last possible drop of wine from the fermenting jar. This often results in pulp being sucked over into the new jar where it can quietly disintegrate, producing appalling off-flavours. Rather than make 4.5 litres (1 gal.) of wine it is better to make 5 litres (9 pt.) so that a clear 4.5 litres (1 gal.) can be racked off unhindered by pulp debris.

**Graves** is a Bordeaux wine, and the best Graves are in fact red wines, but the white Graves appeal greatly to the British palate, so that they are perhaps almost better known than the red wines of this region. Graves is somewhat sweeter than Chablis, and is lower in its acid content. The cheaper wines of this region are sold as Bordeaux Blanc and Bordeaux Superieur, but these are rarely of much account. An interesting experiment can be made by purchasing a bottle of cheap Bordeaux Blanc and comparing it with a good amateur white wine. Except perhaps in the matter of bouquet, which is one of the present weaknesses of amateur winemaking, the commercial product will be found to be inferior to the amateur wine.

The fruits mentioned for simulating Chablis can also be used for Graves, though since Graves has a little more body slightly greater quantities can be used, and in addition small quantities of bananas can be used with advantage. Greengages and yellow plums are also good ingredients for White Bordeaux type wines. A good Bordeaux yeast is required, and the same observations concerning racking will again apply.

**Sauternes** also comes from the Bordeaux region, but it differs from other white wines so much that the Sauternes region is always considered to be distinct from the rest of Bordeaux.

The peculiarity about Sauternes arises from the practice of subjecting the grapes on the vine to the attack of a mould known variously as Botrytis Cinerea, Noble Rot or La Pourriture Noble. This mould, under the right climatic conditions, causes the grape to lose some of their water content, so that both sugar and acid increase. In addition some glycerol (glycerine) is found in the grapes and several other small chemical changes can be observed. The resultant wine is a sweet or very sweet golden dessert wine of overpowering fragrance, with a silkiness and rich flavour that endears itself to connoisseurs as the world's best sweet white wine.

The best Sauternes are superb, culminating in the incomparable **Chateau d'Yquem,** and it would be misleading the reader to suggest that anything approaching these can be fashioned out of the ingredients available to us. Nevertheless, the cheaper types of Sauternes are fairly easy to simulate, provided that the initial must is carefully prepared.

A blend of materials is, of course, required. The basic pattern consists of a light-coloured basic ingredient to which is added either grape concentrate, raisins or sultanas for vinosity. The considerable body and fragrance of Sauternes are best obtained by the addition of bananas and flowers respectively. Small amounts of glycerine can also be added as part of the final sweetening-up procedure prior to bottling, and this will also add the silkiness inherent in Sauternes.

We would like to issue a slight warning at this point on the use of casks. Amateur winemakers tend to use rather small cooperage, 15 or 20 litres (3 gal. or 4½ gal.) casks. Unless these are of very close-grained oak they are **NOT** suitable for maturing white wines except Sauternes even with the protection of considerable amounts of sulphite, for much too much air tends to get to the wine with the result that an oxidised bouquet and taste tend to result. It is better to use polypins and demijohns and to rack the wine at four month intervals with sulphite additions, unless 20 litres (9 gal.) or larger casks are employed.

In the following recipes, the peculiarities of each wine type have been allowed for, but the winemaker will in time realise the principles behind the recipes and be able to design similar recipes for other ingredients he may think suitable. There are many other exciting and interesting wines of France such as those of the Loire Valley, and the winemaker should undertake the fascinating study of these types whenever an opportunity occurs at winetastings and the like. The more one knows about the taste and bouquet of commercial wines, the greater will be one's ability to make good wine. We are not trying blindly to imitate commercial wines, but to produce wines of a **generally similar** nature that will fulfil the same purpose.

72

**Basic procedure**

1. Process ingredients as indicated in recipe.

2. Ferment to dryness, except when making Sauternes type wines, where the sugar additions may be continued in 110 g (¼ lb.) per 4.5 litres (1 gal.) doses 150 ml ((¼ pt.) syrup) until a sweet wine results.

3. When fermentation is finished, rack the wine off the lees into glass containers, sulphite with 100 p.p.m. $SO_2$ (two Campden tablets per 4.5 litres (1 gal.)) and seal with a cork plus fermentation lock, or a cork heavily plugged with cotton wool.

4. Store in a cool place for four months, after which rack again and sulphite as before. In the event of a heavy deposit forming, that might seem to be pulp debris, rack earlier (even as close as a fortnight after the first racking) and add one further Campden tablet per 4.5 litres (1 gal.)

5. Further rackings can be made at four month intervals, and care should be taken to see that the jars are topped up at each racking with wine or water.

6. The wine should become first drinkable at about six months, but will be at its best in one to two years, after which it will hold its quality for a year or two and then gradually decline. Sauternes-type wines may, however, take slightly longer to mature and will certainly retain their quality for several more years before falling into senility.

# Chablis

*Ingredients:*

| | |
|---|---|
| **1.8 kg (4 lb.) green gooseberries** | **450 g (1 lb.) sugar** |
| **570 ml (1 pt.) white grape concentrate** | **15 g (½ oz.) pectinol** |
| **280 ml (½ pt.) elderflowers** | **Nutrients** |
| **Water to 4.5 litres ( 1 gal.)** | **Chablis yeast starter** |

*Method:*

Wash and top and tail the gooseberries. Add the sugar and nutrients to the fruit and add 4 litres (6 pt.) boiling water. When cool add the elderflowers, pectinol and yeast starter. Ferment on the pulp for three days, crushing the fruit by hand daily, then strain off the pulp and press lightly. Add the grape concentrate and sufficient water to make up the volume to 4.5 litres (1 gal.) Thereafter proceed as directed in the basic procedure.

# White Burgundy (1)

*Ingredients:*

1.1 litres (2 pt.) sweet orange juice
570 ml (1 pt.) white grape concentrate
280 ml (½ pt.) elderflowers
675 g (1½ lb.) honey
Nutrients
Burgundy yeast starter
Water to 4.5 litres ( 1 gal.)

*Method:*

Extract the juice from sufficient oranges to give 1.1 litres (2 pt.) juice. Add the grape concentrate, 1.1 litres (2 pt.) water, nutrients, elderflowers and honey and stir until dissolved. Make up to 4 litres (7½ pt.) with water and add the yeast starter. Ferment on the pulp for three days, then strain off the pulp and make the volume up to 4.5 litres (1 gal.) with water. Thereafter continue as instructed in the basic procedure.

# White Burgundy (2)

*Ingredients:*

1.8 kg (4 lb.) apricots
450 g (1 lb.) sultanas
280 ml (½ pt.) yellow rose petals
675 g (1½ lb.) honey

15 g (½ oz.) pectinol
Nutrients
Burgundy yeast starter
Water to 4.5 litres (1 gal.)

*Method:*

Wash and stone the apricots and chop up the sultanas. Add the nutrients and honey and add 4 litres (6 pt.) boiling water. When cool add the rose petals, pectinol and yeast starter. Ferment on the pulp for 2–3 days, then strain off the pulp and press lightly. Make up the volume to 4.5 litres (1 gal.) with water and thereafter proceed as directed in the basic procedure.

# White Burgundy (3)

*Ingredients:*

4.5 kg (10 lb.) green gooseberries
4 litres (6 pt.) orange juice
2.25 litres (4 pt.) white grape conc.
1.1 litres (2 pt.) yellow rose petals
2.25 kg (5 lb.) sugar

30 g (1 oz.) pectinol
Nutrients
Burgundy yeast starter
Water to 20 litres (4½ gal.)

*Method:*

Wash the gooseberries, top and tail and add the nutrients and sugar. Express the juice from sufficient oranges (about 40 oranges) to give 4 litres (6 pt.) juice and add to the gooseberries. Add 10 litres (2½ gal.) boiling water and stir until the sugar, etc., has dissolved. When cool, crush the gooseberries (by hand) and add the pectinol, rose petals and yeast starter. Ferment on the pulp for three days, then strain off the pulp and press lightly. Add the grape concentrate and make the volume up to 20 litres (4½ gal.) with water. Thereafter continue as directed in the basic procedure.

# Sauternes (1)

*Ingredients:*

2.7 kg (6 lb.) yellow plums
900 g (2 lb.) bananas
570 ml (1 pt.) white grape conc.
280 ml (½ pt.) yellow rose petals
15 g (½ oz.) tartaric acid
15 g (½ oz.) malic acid

45 ml (1½ fl. oz. glycerol)
675 g (1½ lb.) sugar
Nutrients
Sauternes yeast starter
Water to 4.5 litres (1 gal.)

*Method:*

Peel the bananas (rejecting the skins) and cut into slices. Boil the slices in 3.5 litres (5 pt.) water for half an hour, then strain carefully over the stoned plums. Add the acids and nutrients while still hot and dissolve the sugar in the hot liquor. When cool, add the rose petals and yeast starter. Ferment on the pulp for 3–4 days, then strain off the pulp and press lightly. Add the grape concentrate and glycerol, dilute to 4.5 litres (1 gal.) with water and thereafter proceed as directed in the basic procedure.

# Sauternes (2)

*Ingredients:*

| | |
|---|---|
| 1.8 kg (4 lb.) parsnips | 45 ml (1½ fl. oz.) glycerol |
| 900 g (2 lb.) bananas | 675 g (1½ lb.) sugar |
| 570 ml (1 pt.) white grape conc. | Nutrients |
| 570 ml (1 pt.) elderflowers | Sauternes yeast starter |
| 15 g (½ oz.) tartaric acid | Water to 4.5 litres (1 gal.) |
| 15 g (½ oz.) malic acid | 15 g (½ oz.) pectinol |

*Method:*

Peel the bananas (rejecting the skins) and cut into slices. Boil the slices together with the washed sliced parsnips in 3 litres (6 pt.) water for half an hour. Strain off carefully and add the nutrients, acids and glycerol to the hot liquor. When cool add the elderflowers, pectinol, white grape concentrate and yeast starter. Ferment on the pulp for two days, then strain off the latter. Add the sugar dissolved in sufficient water to make the volume of the must up to 4.5 litres (1 gal.). Thereafter continue as directed in the basic procedure.

# Sauternes (3)

*Ingredients:*

| | |
|---|---|
| 9 kg (20 lb.) peaches | |
| 4.5 kg (10 lb.) bananas | |
| 2.25 litres (4 pt.) white grape concentrate | |
| 1.1 litres (2 pt.) yellow rose petals | |
| 25 g (¾ oz.) tartaric acid | Nutrients |
| 180 ml (6 fl. oz.) glycerol | Sauternes yeast starter |
| 2.7 kg (6 lb.) honey | Water to 20 litres (4½ gal.) |
| 15 g (½ oz.) malic acid | 30 g (1 oz.) pectinol |

*Method:*

Peel the bananas (rejecting the skins) and cut into slices. Boil the slices in 9 litres (2 gal.) water for half an hour, then strain the hot liquor over the washed stoned peaches. Add the nutrients, acids, glycerol and honey and stir until dissolved. When cool add the rose petals, pectinol and yeast starter. Ferment on the pulp for 2–3 days, then strain off the latter and press lightly. Add the grape concentrate, mix in thoroughly and make up the volume to 20 litres (4½ gal.) with water. Thereafter proceed as instructed in the basic procedure.

# Graves (1)

*Ingredients:*

1.8 kg (4 lb.) sugar beet
570 ml (1 pt.) white grape conc.
280 ml (½ pt.) elderflowers
10 g (½ oz.) tartaric acid

450 g (1 lb.) honey
Nutrients
Bordeaux yeast starter
Water to 4.5 litres (1 gal.)

*Method:*

Wash the sugar beet, cut into chunks and boil in 4 litres (6 pt.) water for half an hour. Strain off the pulp and add the honey, nutrients and acids to the hot liquor. When cool add the elderflowers, grape concentrate and yeast starter. Ferment on the pulp for two days, then strain off the pulp and make up to 4.5 litres (1 gal.) with water. Thereafter continue as directed in the basic procedure.

# Graves (2)

*Ingredients;*

1.8 kg (4 lb.) greengages
900 g (2 lb.) sultanas
280 ml (½ pt.) yellow rose petals
450 g (1 lb.) sugar

Nutrients
Bordeaux yeast starter
Water to 4.5 litres (1 gal.)
15 g (½ oz.) pectinol

*Method:*

Stone the greengages, chop the sultanas and scald with 4 litres (6 pt.) boiling water. Add the sugar and nutrients while still hot and stir until dissolved. When cool add the rose petals, pectinol and yeast starter. Ferment on the pulp for three days, then strain off the latter and press lightly. Make up the volume to 4.5 litres (1 gal.) with the water and thereafter continue as instructed in the basic procedure.

# Graves (3)

*Ingredients:*

900 g (2 lb.) sultanas
1.1 litres (2 pt.) dandelion petals
10 g (¼ oz.) tartaric acid
10 g (¼ oz.) malic acid

900 g (2 lb.) honey
Nutrient
Bordeaux yeast starter
Water to 4.5 litres (1 gal.)

*Method:*

Pick the dandelions on a dry sunny day and cut off the petals, rejecting the green calices. Add 900 g (2 lb.) chopped sultanas to every 1.1 litres (2pt.) petals and add 4.25 litres (7 pt.) boiling water. Add the nutrients, acids and honey and stir until dissolved. When cool add the yeast starter. Ferment on the pulp for two days then strain off the latter and press lightly. Make up the volume to 4.5 litres (1 gal.) with water and thereafter proceed as directed in the basic procedure.

# Graves (4)

*Ingredients:*

1.8 kg (4 lb.) peaches
1.1 litres (2 pt.) gorseflowers
570 ml (1 pt.) white grape conc.
10 g (⅓ oz.) tartaric acid
15 g (½ oz.) pectinol

450 g (1 lb.) honey
Nutrients
Bordeaux yeast starter
Water to 4.5 litres (1 gal.)

*Method:*

Stone the peaches, add the gorseflowers and add 4 litres (6 pt.) boiling water. Add the honey, acid and nutrients until dissolved. When cool add the pectinol, and yeast starter. Ferment on the pulp for three days, then strain off the latter and press lightly. Add the grape concentrate and make the volume up to 4.5 litres (1 gal.) with water. Thereafter proceed as directed in the basic procedure.

# Graves (5)
**(20 litres (4½ gal.))**

*Ingredients:*

9 kg (20 lb.) peaches
1.8 kg (4 lb.) bananas
900 g (2 lb.) raisins
1.1 litres (2 pt.) white grape conc.
1.1 litres (2 pt.) elderflowers
15 g (½ oz.) tartaric acid

15 g (½ oz.) malic acid
1.8 kg (4 lb.) sugar
30 g (1 oz.) pectinol
Nutrients
Bordeaux yeast starter
Water to 20 litres (4½ gal.)

*Method:*

Peel the bananas (rejecting the skins) and cut into slices. Boil the slices in 4.5 litres (1 gal.) water for half an hour, then strain the hot liquor over the stoned peaches and raisins. Add 6 litres (1½ gal.) boiling water and dissolve the acids, nutrients and sugar in the hot liquor. When cool add the elderflowers, pectinol and yeast starter. Ferment on the pulp for three days, then strain off the latter and press lightly. Add the grape concentrate and make the volume up to 20 litres (4½ gal.) with water. Thereafter continue as instructed in the basic procedure.

# Bordeaux Blanc

*Ingredients:*

1.8 kg (4 lb.) parsnips
570 ml (1 pt.) tin pineapple juice
280 ml (½ pt.) white grape conc.
675 g (1½ lb.) honey
5 g (¼ teaspoonful) grape tannin

10 g (¼ oz.) pectinol
10 g (¼ oz.) tartaric acid
Yeast nutrients
Bordeaux yeast starter
Water to 4.5 litres (1 gal.)

*Method:*

Chop and boil parsnips in 3 litres (5 pt.) water for 20 minutes, and strain liquor over pineapple juice, grape concentrate, honey, tannin and acid. When cool add pectinol, yeast nutrient and active yeast starter. Strain off any pulp fragments after three days and thereafter continue as in basic procedure.

# CHAPTER VII

# Chianti: New and Old

Chianti is the best known of Italian wines and as a result there is a tendency to label all Italian dry wines as Chianti. Strictly speaking, however, Chianti comes from the Italian province of Tuscany, the area around the cities of Florence, Pisa, Aretto and Siena.

Life is still somewhat harsh for the Italian peasant, and in his efforts to extract a living from the soil he tends to crowd crops together. Thus vines trained on pergolas are found growing in between other crops, and in fact they are often trained up trees and houses. Wherever there is a space, put in a vine is the policy of most growers, and it does not tend to produce high quality wines. Visitors to Italy will have found that much of this local Chianti has a rough astringent taste, with a grip on the tongue as though one were chewing oak bark. This is old-style Chianti – some people like it – for it can become an acquired taste, so we have included some recipes in this section.

The leading Tuscan growers have, however, made strenuous efforts in recent years to raise the standard of Chianti to a much higher level. These new-style Chiantis are much smoother, full-bodied, dry wines and are more refined than the older style types although in many cases they are still a little more astringent than comparable French red wines. They are often bottled in ordinary wine bottles rather than in the wickered flagons that one normally associates with Chianti.

Their labels bear the emblems of a black cock on a gold background. To produce wine of this type is not too difficult, and once the correct blend of ingredients is chosen there are no special techniques involved. The normal winemaking procedure is all that is necessary.

White Chiantis exist in large numbers, but because they are not rated very highly we have not made provision for recipes of this type. In the main these wines are indistinguishable from any of the carafe wines one comes across anywhere in Europe.

*The typical, straw-encased Chianti bottle.*

### Sparkling

There is, however, one additional type of Chianti that deserves some attention. These wines are called Frizzante, a name which indicates they are sparkling, "Italian Bubbly" in fact. They are, nevertheless, not frothy like champagne, for that superb wine Asti Spumante fulfils that role. They are made by what is called the Governo process. In this process small amounts of fresh grape juice are added to the wine just when the fermentation is all but finished. The wine is bottled shortly after this, so that a very small secondary fermentation occurs inside the bottle. Of course, since the wine is not dealt with in the manner of champagne, there is a small yeast deposit in each bottle, but no one seems to mind if the last couple of glasses are a little cloudy. Indeed, yeast is said to be excellent for the complexion and these glasses are often given to the ladies on this pretext.

# Warning

A hydrometer is essential for the production of Frizzante wines and we would not recommend anyone trying to make them without its aid, in case exploding bottles are the result. There are in fact three ways one can approach the problem. Firstly, one can follow the Italian method, and add syrup or grape concentrate when the fermentation is finished and one has ascertained with the hydrometer that the specific gravity has fallen well below the 1000 mark.

The amount to add would be 150 ml (¼ pt.) of grape concentrate or syrup that has a gravity of 48 to each 4.5 litres (1 gal.) of wine.

This addition should be made about three to four weeks after the first racking and the wine is then immediately racked once more and bottled with ordinary straight wine corks, but the corks should not be wired down. The bottles should be stored upright in case a slight error of judgment has occurred and the corks blow out.

The second method is to rack the wine when it has fallen just below the 1000 mark and to sulphite the wine with 50 parts per million (1 Campden tablet per 4.5 litres (1 gal.)), leave the wine for a few days to clear somewhat, and then to bottle. There is slightly more risk of corks blowing out here and they must be watched and replaced if they do.

Do not tie the corks but just replace them. Eventually the amount of carbon dioxide will be insufficient to force out the corks while still being enough to provide a sparkle.

The safest way to ensure the right amount of sugar is to test the wine after racking with a Clinitest outfit (available from chemists). This is a simple outfit used by diabetics and with its help one can tell in a few seconds what percentage of sugar is left in the wine. The wine should be bottled when the outfit indicates that between ¼ per cent and ½ per cent is left in the wine.

## Basic Method

(In the recipes that follow, quantities are given for 20 litres (4½ gal.) ferments, since for all dry red wines it is best to make this quantity at least and to mature the wine in a cask. The quantities should be scaled down accordingly if 4.5 litres (1 gal.) are required as would normally be the case for Frizzante wines).

1. Prepare ingredients as indicated in each recipe.

2. When fermentation has ceased the wine should be racked off the lees into a fresh container, preferably a cask, and thereafter be racked every four months. Evaporation losses can be replaced with water or a mixture of water and wine. The wine should be matured in this way for at least six months for an old-style Chianti or a year for a new-style Chianti before bottling.

3. If a Frizzante wine is required proceed in one of the following ways:

  (a) Test fermentation with a hydrometer and when below 1000 (say 995) add one Campden tablet per 4.5 litres (1 gal.), rack and bottle four to seven days later, leaving 25 mm (1½ in.) below the cork. Store in a cool place and check corks daily for a week or so and then occasionally, replacing them if they blow out. Wine should be kept a year before drinking.

  (b) Test fermenting wine in its final stages with a Clinitest outfit and when colour test indicates a green result (¼ to ½% sugar) rack and bottle as before.

  (c) Test fermenting wine with a hydrometer, rack when it falls below the 1000 mark, rack again three weeks later and add syrup or grape concentrate of gravity 48 (approximately 110 g

(¼ lb.) sugar boiled up with 570 ml (1 pt.) of water) at the rate of 150 ml (¼ pt.) of this syrup to each 4.5 litres (1 gal.) Bottle as before.

## RECIPE 1 (Old-style)

(Frizzante wines can be made from any of the following recipes).
*Ingredients:*

4 kg (9 lb.) elderberries
4 kg (9 lb.) raisins      Yeast nutrients
1.1 litres (2 pt.) red grape conc.      Chianti yeast starter
1.8 kg (4 lb.) honey      Water to 20 litres (4½ gal.)

*Method:*

Crush the elderberries and raisins and scald with 15 litres (3½ gal.) of boiling water. Stir in the honey and yeast nutrients. When cool add the yeast starter and ferment on the pulp for three days. Strain off the pulp and press lightly. Add the grape concentrate and make up the volume to 20 litres (4½ gal.) with cold water. Thereafter proceed as directed in the basic procedure.

## RECIPE 2 (Old-style)

*Ingredients:*

6.25 kg (14 lb.) damsons      30 g (1 oz.) pectinol
1.3 kg (3 lb.) bananas      Yeast nutrients
1.1 litres (2 pt.) red grape conc.      Chianti yeast starter
2.7 kg (6 lb.) sugar      Water to 20 litres (4½ gal.)

*Method:*

Peel the bananas (rejecting the skins) and cut into slices. Boil the slices in 4.5 litres (1 gal.) water for half an hour and then strain the hot liquor over the stoned damsons. Add 10 litres (2½ gal.) of boiling water and stir in the sugar and yeast nutrients. When cool add the pectinol and yeast starter. Ferment on the pulp for four to five days, then strain off the pulp and press lightly. Add the grape concentrate and make up the volume to 20 litres (4½ gal.) with cold water. Thereafter continue as instructed in the basic procedure.

84

*An Italian girl treading her own grapes in a London garden.*

**RECIPE 3 (New-style)**

*Ingredients:*

| | |
|---|---|
| 8 kg (18 lb.) cherries | 1.8 kg (4 lb.) sugar or honey |
| 1.8 kg (4 lb.) raisins | Yeast nutrients |
| 1.3 kg (3 lb.) bananas | Chianti yeast starter |
| 1.1 litres (2 pt.) red grape conc. | Water to 20 litres (4½ gal.) |

*Method:*

Peel the bananas (rejecting the skins) and cut into slices. Boil the slices in about 4.5 litres (1 gal.) of water for half an hour, then strain the hot liquor over the washed, crushed cherries and raisins (cherry stones should not be broken). Add a further 9 litres (2 gal.) of boiling water together with the sugar or honey and yeast nutrients and stir until dissolved. When cool add the yeast starter. Ferment on the pulp for four to five days, then strain off the pulp and press lightly. Add the grape concentrate and make up the volume to 20 litres (4½ gal.) with cold water. Thereafter continue as instructed in the basic procedure.

**RECIPE 4 (New-style)**

*Ingredients:*

| | |
|---|---|
| 900 g (2 lb.) dried elderberries | 2.25 kg (5 lb.) honey |
| 900 g (2 lb.) dried bilberries | Yeast nutrients |
| 900 g (2 lb.) raisins | Chianti yeast starter |
| 1.1 litres (2 pt.) red grape conc. | Water to 20 litres (4½ gal.) |

*Method:*

Wash the elderberries, bilberries and raisins and scald with 15 litres (3½ gal.) boiling water. Add the honey and yeast nutrients and stir until the honey has dissolved. When cool add the yeast starter. Ferment on the pulp for two days, then strain off and pulp and press lightly. Add the grape concentrate and make up the volume to 20 litres (4½ gal.) with cold water. Thereafter proceed as directed in the basic procedure.

## RECIPE 5 (Old-style)

*Ingredients:*

| | |
|---|---|
| 4.5 kg (10 lb.) sloes | 2.25 kg (5 lb.) sugar or honey |
| 1.8 kg (4 lb.) bananas | Yeast nutrients |
| 900 g (2 lb.) raisins | Chianti yeast starter |
| 1.1 litres (2 pt.) red grape conc. | Water to 20 litres (4½ gal.) |

*Method:*

Peel the bananas (reject the skins) and cut into slices. Boil the slices in about 4.5 litres (1 gal.) water for half an hour, then strain the hot liquor over the washed, crushed sloes and raisins. Add another 9 litres (2 gal.) boiling water, together with the sugar or honey and yeast nutrients and stir until dissolved. When cool add the yeast starter. Ferment on the pulp for two-three days, then strain off the pulp and press lightly. Add the grape concentrate and make up the volume to 20 litres (4½ gal.) with cold water. Thereafter continue as directed in the basic procedure.

## RECIPE 6 (New-style)

*Ingredients:*

| | |
|---|---|
| 8 kg (18 lb.) elderberries | |
| 1.8 kg (4 lb.) bananas | Yeast nutrients |
| 2.2 litres (4 pt.) red grape conc. | Chianti yeast starter |
| 1.3 kg (3 lb.) honey or sugar | Water to 20 litres (4½ gal.) |

*Method:*

Crush the elderberries and strain off the juice, keeping the pulp. Peel the bananas (reject the skins) and cut into slices. Boil the slices in 4.5 litres (1 gal.) water for half an hour, then strain the hot liquor over the elderberry pulp. Stir the latter for five minutes, then strain. Add another 4.5 litres (1 gal.) of boiling water to the elderberry pulp, stir for five minutes and again strain. Reject the elderberry pulp. Add another 4.5 litres (1 gal.) of water to the banana and elderberry extract together with the honey or sugar and yeast nutrients, and stir until dissolved. When cool add the grape concentrate, sufficient water to bring the volume up to 20 litres (4½ gal.) and the yeast starter. Ferment in the normal manner and finally proceed as directed in the basic procedure.

# CHAPTER VIII

# Romantic Madeira, Bual, Malmsey

Madeira is a romantic wine, for the Portuguese island from which it takes its name is itself a largely unspoilt paradise with an ideal climate, a place of beautiful mountain ranges and lush vegetation. Many of the old ways are still in vogue, and it is a common sight to see the freshly fermented wine being carried down the hillside in goatskins on the backs of carriers.

Madeira is really a group of four wines, and together they can cater with a complete meal from Aperitif to Liqueur. The amber wine Sercial is the driest and has a nutty flavour that makes it an ideal aperitif. Next follows Verdelho, a golden coloured wine that is a little sweeter than Sercial but has an aromatic bouquet that renders it suitable either as an aperitif or as a table wine. Bual, on the other hand, is a full-bodied medium sweet tawny wine that is suitable for dessert or for general drinking. The last of the four, Malmsey, is perhaps the best known of the four types and was much loved by the English Court circles in earlier days. It is a very lush deep tawny wine that can easily serve as a liqueur in discerning company.

In order to produce wines of the Madeira type, one needs the right ingredients, the right technique and a certain amount of luck. The technique that is used to produce these wonderful wines of Madeira will normally ruin the wines of other lands, and similarly, any lack of balance in the amateur winemaker's must may equally well produce a failure to some extent. However, it must be admitted that when things go right the resultant Madeira-type wine is well worth the risk.

The range of ingredients from which Madeira type wines can be made is a little limited and is primarily confined to the following: Bananas, Raisins, Grape concentrate, Sultanas, Sugar Beet, Yellow

*Matured Madeira ready for shipment.*

Plums, Greengages, Peaches and Parsnips. If the reader is contemplating some other ingredient, it might well be suitable if it is not a deep red colour (except perhaps blackberries which lose their colour fairly quickly) and if it does not have too much flavour of its own.

Next, an essential for success is a good Madeira yeast and a fermentation that is nurtured most carefully, with sugar additions (in syrup form) in very small doses. An ideal fermenting temperature is around 20°C (70°F) but after a few days a temperature of 17°C (65°F) is even better, for this will ensure a long slow fermentation (in Madeira this lasts as long as ten weeks before racking). Under these conditions 18% alcohol by volume (31° Proof) can be obtained without too much difficulty.

## Estufagem

Once the wine has fermented out, and has been racked into fresh containers there follows the estufagem process, which really means that the wine is heated for a long period.

**The temperatures used in Madeira are as follows:—**
**Best wines 32–38°C (90–100°F) for up to a year.**
**Superior wines 38–43°C (100–110°F) for 6 months.**
**Ordinary grades 49°C (120°F) for 4½ months.**
**Cheapest wines 54–60°C (130–140°F) for 3 months.**

For the amateur winemaker, his "estufa" or baking chamber is anywhere where one of these temperatures can be maintained for the required time. Ideally the temperature should not vary at all from day to day, but with the robust ingredients in our wines this is less important than when dealing with the grape alone. Some people have a stove or radiator which is always hot in winter and above which the wine can be stored. A lagged box heated with an electric light bulb, such as used by amateur tobacco growers for curing, will also suffice. Given a "non-English" summer an outside greenhouse or cold frame will do if the wine is wrapped up at night with a bit of blanket. A thermostatically controlled fermentation cupboard in which a constant temperature can be maintained indefinitely is, of course, ideal for the purpose.

The wine is simply left in these temperatures in demijohn jars (allowing for a little expansion and for a temporary renewal of fermentation until the yeast is killed by the heat). Evaporation losses are very small but a miniature brandy per 4.5 litres (1 gal.) can be used to top up the small amount of lost alcohol.

# Awful!

When the wine has finished its baking, it must be racked into fresh containers. At this stage it will, and should, taste awful. Many off-flavours will have occurred, and most of these will become sublimated into finer flavours given time. Only one of these off-flavours requires any treatment and that is the burnt sugar taste caused by excess caramelisation of some residual sugar. This is easily cured by using the ageing compound "Senex" or alternatively by obtaining some charcoal from a chemists and this is added to the wine for a few days (about 15–30 g (½–1 oz.) per 4.5 litres (1 gal.)), after which the wine is again racked and left to mature.

This wine does require a fair amount of maturing and should not be made with the idea of early drinking. Cask maturing is of course better once one has acquired the technique and can risk larger quantities.

## Basic Procedure for Madeira-Type Wines

1. Proceed as directed in the recipe for the preparation of the must.

2. Check the gravity of the must regularly and add 150 ml (¼ pt.) sugar syrup per 4.5 litres (1 gal.) whenever the gravity drops to 5 or less. This syrup is made by boiling up 900 g (2 lb.) sugar with 570 ml (1 pt.) of water. For Sercial or Verdelho do not add more sugar syrup when fermentation slows down to the extent that a gravity drop of only 12 per day is occuring. This will ensure a dry wine. For Bual and Malmsey wines the sugar syrup additions should be continued until fermentation ceases and a sweet wine is obtained.

3. When fermentation has ceased, allow the wine to settle for a few days, and then rack into demijohn jars.

4. Place the jars in a warm place, at one of the temperatures described in the article and for the required time. There may be a little initial frothing for a few hours, after which the jar can be topped up and left until the estufagem process has been completed.

5. Then rack into fresh jars or into casks and add 10–30 g (¼–1 oz.) charcoal per 4.5 litres (1 gal.) for three days.

6. Rack again, and mature until the wine is ready for drinking, which in some cases may be as long as two years.

# Sercial or Verdelho
## RECIPE 1
*Ingredients:*

1.3 kg (3 lb.) plums or greengages
675 g (1½ lb.) bananas
570 ml (1 pt.) white grape conc.
15 g (½ oz.) tartaric acid
15 g (½ oz.) pectinol

Yeast nutrients
Madeira yeast starter
Sugar as required
Water to 4.5 litres (1 gal.)

*Method*

Peel the bananas and cut into slices (reject the skins). Boil the slices in 3 litres (5 pt.) water for ½ hour, then strain the hot liquor over the stoned plums or greengages. Add the tartaric acid and nutrients. When cool add the pectinol and yeast starter. Ferment on the pulp for 3–4 days then strain off and press the pulp. Add the grape concentrate and sufficient sugar syrup to bring the volume up to about 4 litres (7 pt.). Thereafter procedure is directed as outlined in the basic method.

# Sercial or Verdelho
## RECIPE 2
*Ingredients:*

2 litres (3 pt.) dandelion petals
900 g (2 lb.) bananas
570 ml (1 pt.) white grape conc.
450 g (1 lb.) honey
15 g (½ oz.) tartaric acid

Yeast nutrients
Madeira yeast starter
Sugar as required
Water to 4.5 litres (1 gal.)

*Method:*

Peel the bananas and cut into slices (reject the skins). Boil the slices in 3 litres (5 pt.) of water for half an hour, then strain the hot liquor over the dandelion petals and honey. Add the tartaric acid and nutrients. When cool mix in 280 ml (½ pt.) grape concentrate and add the yeast starter. Ferment on the flowers for two days then strain off the pulp and press lightly. Add the rest of the grape concentrate and sufficient sugar syrup to bring the volume up to about 4 litres (7 pt.). Thereafter continue as detailed in the basic procedure.

# Sercial or Verdelho

## RECIPE 3
*Ingredients:*

| | |
|---|---|
| **1.8 kg (4 lb.) peaches** | |
| **450 g (1 lb.) bananas** | **Yeast nutrients** |
| **675 g (1½ lb.) raisins** | **Madeira yeast starter** |
| **20 g (¾ oz.) tartaric acid** | **Sugar as required** |
| **15 g (½ oz.) pectinol** | **Water to 4.5 litres (1 gal.)** |

*Method:*

Peel the bananas and cut into slices (reject the skins). Boil the slices in 3 litres (5 pt.) of water for half an hour, then strain the hot liquor over the washed raisins and stoned peaches. Add the tartaric acid and nutrients. When cool add the pectinol and yeast starter. Ferment on the pulp for three days then strain off and press the pulp. Bring the volume up to about 4 litres (7 pt.) with sugar syrup and water and then continue as instructed in the basic procedure.

# Sercial or Verdelho

## RECIPE 4
*Ingredients:*

| | |
|---|---|
| **1.8 kg (4 lb.) ripe gooseberries** | |
| **900 g (2 lb.) bananas** | **Yeast nutrients** |
| **570 ml (1 pt.) white grape conc.** | **Madeira yeast starter** |
| **10 g (¼ oz.) tartaric acid** | **Sugar as required** |
| **15 g (½ oz.) pectinol** | **Water to 4.5 litres (1 gal.)** |

*Method:*

Peel the bananas and cut into slices (reject the skins). Boil the slices in 3 litres (5 pt.) of water for half an hour, then strain the hot liquor over the crushed gooseberries. Add the tartaric acid and nutrients. When cool add 280 ml (½ pt.) of grape concentrate, the pectinol and the yeast starter. Ferment on the pulp for three days then strain off and press the pulp. Add the other 280 ml (½ pt.) of grape concentrate and sufficient sugar syrup to bring the volume up to about 4 litres (7 pt.). Thereafter proceed as directed in the basic procedure.

# Sercial or Verdelho

**(20 litres cask maturing)**

**RECIPE 5**
*Ingredients:*
    **4.5 kg (10 lb.) peaches**
    **4.5 kg (10 lb.) ripe gooseberries**
    **4.25 kg (9 lb.) bananas**
    **900 g (2 lb.) raisins**
    **3.3 litres (3 pt.) white grape concentrate**
    **30 g (1 oz.) tartaric acid**
    **30 g (1 oz.) pectinol**
    **Yeast nutrients**
    **Madeira yeast starter**
    **Sugar as required**
    **Water to 20 litres (4½ gal.)**

*Method:*
    Peel the bananas and cut into slices (reject the skins). Boil the slices in 10 litres (2½ gal.) water for half an hour, then strain the hot liquor over the stoned peaches, crushed gooseberries and washed raisins. Add the tartaric acid and nutrients. When cool mix in 570 ml (1 pt.) of grape concentrate and add the pectinol and yeast starter. Ferment on the pulp for three days, then strain off and press the pulp. Add the rest of the grape concentrate and sufficient sugar syrup to bring the volume up to about 18 litres (3¾ gal.). Thereafter proceed as instructed in the basic procedure. Cask maturing after heat treatment (and charcoal treatment if necessary) is recommended.

94

# Sercial or Verdelho

**(20 litres cask maturing)**

**RECIPE 6**

*Ingredients:*

    **8 kg (18 lb.) greengages or yellow plums**
    **4.5 kg (9 lb.) bananas**
    **165 g (3 pkt.) dried dandelion petals**
    **900 g (2 lb.) raisins**
    **3.3 litres (3 pt.) white grape concentrate**
    **45 g (1½ oz.) tartaric acid**
    **30 g (1 oz.) pectinol**
    **Yeast nutrients**
    **Madeira yeast starter**
    **Sugar as required**
    **Water to 20 litres (4½ gal.)**

*Method:*

Peel the bananas and cut into slices (reject the skins). Boil the slices in 10 litres (2½ gal.) water for half an hour then strain the hot liquor over the dandelion petals, washed raisins and stoned greengages. Add the tartaric acid and nutrients. When cool, add the pectinol and yeast starter. Ferment on the pulp for three days then strain off and press the pulp. Add the grape concentrate and sufficient sugar syrup to bring the volume up to 18 litres (3¾ gal.). Thereafter continue as directed in the basic procedure. Cask maturing after heat treatment (and charcoal treatment if necessary) is recommended.

# Bual or Malmsey

**RECIPE 7**

*Ingredients:*

| | |
|---|---|
| **2.7 kg (6 lb.) blackberries** | **Yeast nutrients** |
| **900 g (2 lb.) bananas** | **Madeira yeast starter** |
| **570 ml (1 pt.) white grape conc.** | **Sugar as required** |
| **15 g (½ oz.) pectinol** | **Water to 4.5 litres (1 gal.)** |

*Method:*

Peel the bananas and cut into slices (reject the skins). Boil the slices in 3 litres (5 pt.) water for half an hour and then strain the hot liquor over the crushed blackberries. Add the nutrients. When cool add the pectinol and yeast starter. Ferment on the pulp for two days and then strain off and press pulp lightly. Add the grape concentrate and sufficient sugar syrup to bring the volume up to about 4 litres (7 pt.). Thereafter proceed as instructed in the basic procedure.

# Bual or Malmsey

## RECIPE 8
*Ingredients:*

1.8 kg (4 lb.) parsnips
900 g (2 lb.) bananas        **Yeast nutrients**
570 ml (1 pt.) white grape conc.    **Madeira yeast starter**
15 g (½ oz.) tartaric acid      **Sugar as required**
15 g (½ oz.) pectinol       **Water to 4.5 litres (1 gal.)**

*Method:*

Peel the bananas and cut into slices (reject the skins). Boil the slices in 3 litres (5 pt.) water for half an hour together with the washed sliced parsnips. Strain off carefully and add the tartaric acid and nutrients. When cool add the grape concentrate, pectinol and yeast starter together with sufficient sugar syrup to bring the volume up to about 4 litres (7 pt.). Thereafter proceed as directed in the basic procedure.

# Bual or Malmsey

## RECIPE 9
*Ingredients:*

2.7 kg (6 lb.) ripe gooseberries
900 g (2 lb.) bananas       **Yeast nutrients**
900 g (2 lb.) raisins        **Madeira yeast starter**
10 g (¼ oz.) tartaric acid     **Sugar as required**
10 g (¼ oz.) pectinol       **Water to 4.5 litres (1 gal.)**

*Method:*

Peel the bananas and cut into slices (reject the skins). Boil the slices in 3 litres (5 pt.) water for half an hour then strain the hot liquor over the washed raisins and crushed gooseberries. Add the nutrients and tartaric acid. When cool add the pectinol and yeast starter. Ferment on the pulp for three days then strain off the pulp and press lightly. Add 280 ml (½ pt.) water and sufficient sugar syrup to bring the volume up to about 4 litres (7 pt.). Thereafter continue as directed in the basic procedure.

# Bual or Malmsey

**RECIPE 10**

*Ingredients:*

**900 g (2 lb.) bananas**
**450 g (1 lb.) dried apricots**
**570 ml (1 pt.) white grape concentrate**
**15 g (½ oz.) pectinol**
**Yeast nutrients**
**Madeira yeast starter**
**Sugar as required**
**Water to 4.5 litres (1 gal.)**

*Method:*

Peel the bananas and cut into slices (reject the skins). Boil the slices and dried apricots in 3 litres (5 pt.) water for half an hour, then strain off and press lightly. Add the nutrients and when cool add the pectinol and yeast starter. After two days add the grape concentrate and sufficient sugar syrup to bring the volume up to about 4 litres (7 pt.). Thereafter proceed as instructed in the basic procedure.

# Malmsey or Bual

**(20 litres cask maturing)**

**RECIPE 11**

*Ingredients:*

8 kg (18 lb.) peaches
4 kg (9 lb.) ripe gooseberries
4 kg ( 9lb.) bananas
1.8 kg (4 lb.) raisins
1.1 litres (2 pt.) white grape concentrate
1.8 kg (4 lb.) honey
15 g (½ oz.) tartaric acid
30 g (1 oz.) pectinol
**Nutrients**
**Madeira yeast starter**
**Sugar as required**
**Water to 20 litres (4½ gal.)**

*Method:*

Peel the bananas and cut into slices (reject the skins). Boil the slices in about 13 litres (2¾ gal.) water for half an hour, then strain the hot liquor over the crushed gooseberries, stoned peaches, washed raisins and honey. Add the tartaric acid and nutrients. When cool add the pectinol and yeast starter. Ferment on the pulp for 3 days and then strain off and press the pulp lightly. Add the grape concentrate and sufficient sugar syrup to bring the volume up to about 18 litres (3¾ gal.). Thereafter proceed as directed in the basic procedure. Cask maturing after heat treatment is recommended.

# CHAPTER IX

# Rosé Wines

One often is asked about Vin Rosé, and it is a type of wine which seems to stir people's imagination. Its beautiful colour, ranging from delicate pink to almost red, goes well with both sunlight and candlelight, so that it is equally acceptable in summer or winter. Also, it can be drunk at almost any time of day with satisfaction, and in quantity without undue intoxication.

We have a friend, blind from birth, who recently started making wine. In order to give him an idea of the types of wines he might expect from different ingredients a tasting was arranged, in the course of which he tasted both white and red wines and quickly discerned their difference in character by taste alone, since red and white meant nothing to him. On being given a rosé wine he remarked that it did not differ very much from the white wines and was certainly quite unlike the reds.

This profound observation was once often rediscovered by wine judges when encountering a rosé wine among a class of red wines. The unfortunate rosé was so different from the rest of the class that it rarely stood a chance of gaining an award. This anomaly has had to be resolved, and rosé wines are now usually assigned a separate class of their own.

Most winemaking areas of Europe produce rosé wines and apart from minor local practices the method of production is fundamentally the same. It is based on the fact that the colouring matter in a grape is generally localised in the skin and does not dissolve easily in grape juice although it does so quite readily in dilute solutions of alcohol such as fermenting wine musts. Thus, if either red or white grapes are pressed the juice expressed is white and a white wine will result. If, however, black grapes are fermented on the pulp, the must rapidly darkens in colour and after about four or five days of such fermentation, enough colour has been extracted to make the finished wine deep red. At the same time, a considerable amount of tannin is extracted which gives a red wine its characteristic "bite". Rosé wines are made in the same way, but the period of pulp fermentation is restricted to a period varying between 6 hours and 48 hours according to the degree of pinkness and astringency required.

There are other ways of producing rosé wines but nearly always these produce wines of an inferior quality. For instance, in some parts of Europe vin rosé is made simply by blending a white wine with a small proportion of red wine. Such a blend rarely marries well and a lack of homogeneity is recognised when tasting the wine. It is even possible to make vin rosé from a certain type of grape called a teinturier which has a reddish-purple pulp and yields a reddish juice. This type of vin rosé is quite common in Algeria but very little of it is exported.

Some of the best rosé wines, mostly quite light in colour, are produced in the Loire valley of France, those of Anjou, Saumur and Touraine being the best known. They are good honest wines bottled about six months after fermentation in order to preserve their freshness and fragrance and generally drunk within the year, although they tend to improve for a further two years. They are mostly made from Cabernet or Groslot grapes, although there is a wine, Pinot Rosé de Sancerre (made from Pinot Noir grapes), which is very much sought after and is quite difficult to obtain in this country.

Wines of a similar nature are made in the Basses Pyrenees (rosé de Béarn) and in Portugal where the increasingly popular Mateus Rosé is produced. This latter wine is gaining popularity through its sheer merit rather than through any form of advertising, and it has the additional attraction of being slightly sparkling, not effervescent like Champagne but with bubbles hugging the sides of the glass, and a slightly prickly taste.

Deeper coloured rosé wines are produced in the Burgundy district, further south in the Rhône valley and generally in the Mediterranean area (Algeria, Corsica, Yugoslavia, Spain and Portugal). In most cases the period of pulp fermentation extends to 48 hours, varying with local practice and the type of grape. Many of these are either poor in quality or made in such small quantities that they rarely reach this country. However, one exception is Tavel Rosé, said by some to be the finest rosé wine in the world. It is made from a variety of cépages, notably the Grenache and Cinsault vines which with others are used in making the great red wine of the Rhône valley – Châteauneuf-du-Pape.

A very deep rosé called Clairet is made in the Bordeaux region. It is typical of the type of Bordeaux shipped to this country during the Middle Ages before the much superior Claret was produced. This type of wine (labelled Clairet, Bordeaux Rosé or simply Vin Rosé) is of interest in that it provides a useful standard of comparison for the amateur even though it is of no great interest commercially. If the winemaker can produce rosé wines of comparable quality, he can rest assured in his ability in this field of winemaking.

The problem facing amateur winemakers is not in producing a pink or light red wine, for this is extremely simple. The difficulty is in achieving the fresh fruity flavour and bouquet associated with rosé wines. This fruity freshness is, however, not strongly reminiscent of the ingredients of the must, but rather a characteristic of a fairly young wine. Having achieved these factors, of course, great care is necessary to avoid losing them again during racking and maturing.

Fruits which lend themselves well to this "fruity" aspect of rosé wine production are red-currants, rhubarb, apricots, cherries, green gooseberries, peaches, rosehips, and white grape concentrate. Strawberries are also of use provided cold extraction methods are used in preparing the must and great care given to the finished wine. The rosé colour can be achieve or intensified best by the addition of a little red grape concentrate.

Most rosé wines are around 10–11% alcohol by volume and quite lose their character if made any stronger, so that a starting gravity of about 80 only is required. The acidity of the pink rosés of the Loire type is between 3.5 and 4.0 p.p.t. (in terms of sulphuric acid measurement) but the majority of the acid present is malic and this type of wine cannot be made if this acidity is achieved with the harsher tasting acids tartaric and citric alone. The acidity of the deeper coloured rosés is lower (between 3.0 and 3.5 p.p.t) but here the greater part of the acid is tartaric, the remainder being malic.

Care in handling the fermentation is perhaps the most important factor once a suitable blend of fruits is available. Cold water extraction or pressing is practically essential and this in turn involves the use of sulphite (Campden tablets). A fairly cool fermentation 18–22°C (65–70°F) is a distinct advantage to avoid dissipation of fragrance. Since this may involve a slightly longer period of fermentation, it is necessary to make sure that the initial must is as "clean" as possible, i.e. does not contain pulp fragments which might disintegrate during the fermentation period. Racking also should be done very carefully, with not too great a distance between the two jars and without splashing. At each racking the wine should be sulphited with a Campden tablet per gallon (50 p.p.m.) at least – some commercial rosés being kept almost permanently under 75 p.p.m. $SO_2$ during the whole period of their maturing. Generally, the finished wines should be bottled for two or three months at least before being consumed. This allows the last vestiges of sulphur dioxide to vanish and for the natural bouquet and flavour to reassert itself. The wine is best lightly chilled before being consumed.

Finally, a good case can be made out for the use of a pectin-destroying enzyme preparation such as Rohament P, Pectinol or Pektolase in making these wines. The period of maturing is so short, in order to preserve the fruity freshness, that there is no time to be lost in obtaining a brilliantly clear wine. Filtration would be disastrous to such a wine and even finings leave much to be desired in this case. It is infinitely preferable to add a small quantity of one of the above-mentioned preparations to the must at the same time as entering the yeast. A level teaspoonful of the enzyme preparation per 4.5 litres (1 gal.) is quite sufficient at this stage and one does not have to resort to the more massive additions sometimes required to clear a finished wine that is hazy.

## Basic Procedure

1. Process ingredients as indicated in recipe.
2. Store the finished wine in a cool place and rack again when it is three months old and again three months later. At each racking care should be taken to avoid splashing, the wine should be sulphited with 1 or 2 Campden tablets per 4.5 litres (1 gal.) and the jar should be topped up with wine or water. In the event of a heavy deposit forming that might seem to be pulp debris, rack earlier (even as close as a fortnight after the first racking) and add one further Campden tablet per 4.5 litres (1 gal.)

3. When the wine is six months old, it should be sulphited with 50 p.p.m. $SO_2$ (1 Campden tablet per 4.5 litres (1 gal.)) and bottled.

4. The finished wine should be drinkable at this stage, but will normally improve in bottle for a further 18 months.

## RECIPE 1

*Ingredients:*

**1.8 kg (4 lb.) red-currants**
**570 ml (1 pt.) white grape concentrate**
**280 ml (½ pt.) red rose petals**
**Nutrients**
**Bordeaux yeast**
**550 g (1¼ lb.) clover honey**
**Water to 4.5 litres (1 gal.)**

*Method:*

Crush the red-currants and add 3.5 litres (6 pt.) cold water in which the honey and nutrients have been dissolved. Add 100 p.p.m. sulphite (2 Campden tablets) and leave covered for 24 hours before introducing the yeast starter. Ferment on the pulp for three days and then strain it off and press lightly. Add the grape concentrate and make the volume up to 4.5 litres (1 gal.) with water. After another four days add the rose petals and ferment on the flowers for three days before straining them off. The wine at this stage should possess a good rosé colour. Rack for the first time when the gravity drops to just below 0, add 50 p.p.m. sulphite (1 Campden tablet) and rack again as soon as fermentation restarts or a heavy deposit forms, whichever is the sooner. Thereafter proceed as directed in the basic procedure.

## RECIPE 2

*Ingredients;*

**1.8 kg (4 lb.) green gooseberries**
**280 ml (½ pt.) red grape conc.**
**280 ml (½ pt.) elderflowers**
**Nutrients**

**Bordeaux yeast**
**675 g (1½ lb.) sugar**
**Water to 4.5 litres (1 gal.)**

*Method:*

Top and tail the gooseberries and add 3.5 litres (6 pt.) hot water together with the sugar and nutrients. Add 100 p.p.m. sulphite (2 Campden tablets) and leave covered for 24 hours. After this time, the gooseberries will have softened and should be crushed before introducing the yeast starter. Ferment on the pulp for three days, then strain it off and press lightly. Add the grape concentrate and make the volume up to 4.5 litres (1 gal.) with water. After another four days, add the elderflower and ferment on the flowers for three days before straining them off. Rack for the first time at a gravity of 0, add 50 p.p.m. sulphite (1 Campden tablet) and there-after proceed as directed in the basic procedure.

## RECIPE 3

*Ingredients:*

**900 g (2 lb.) peaches**
**450 g (1 lb.) elderberries**
**280 ml (½ pt.) white grape concentrate**
**280 ml (½ pt.) red rose petals**
**675 g (1½ lb.) sugar**
**Nutrients**
**Burgundy yeast**
**Water to 4.5 litres (1 gal.)**

*Method:*

Stone the peaches and press out the juice. Crush the elderberries and add to the peach juice. Add 3 litres (5 pt.) water, in which the nutrients and sugar have been dissolved and sulphite 100 p.p.m. (2 Campden tablets). After 24 hours, introduce the yeast and ferment on the pulp until a light to medium rosé colour develops (1–2 days) then strain off the pulp and press it lightly. After four-five days, add the grape concentrate and rose petals and ferment on the latter for two-three days depending upon how deep a rosé colour is desired. When the flowers are removed, make up the volume to 4.5 litres (1 gal.) with water and ferment to a gravity of just below 0. Rack at this stage, add 50 p.p.m. sulphite (1 Campden tablet) and thereafter proceed as directed in the basic procedure.

## RECIPE 4

*Ingredients:*

110 g (4 oz.) dried rosehip shells
450 g (1 lb.) sultanas
280 ml (½ pt.) red grape conc.
280 ml (½ pt.) elderflowers
10 g (¼ oz.) tartaric acid

450 g (1 lb.) sugar
Nutrients
Bordeaux yeast
10 g (¼ oz.) malic acid
Water to 4.5 litres (1 gal.)

*Method:*

Wash the rosehips and sultanas and add 3.5 litres (6 pt.) water containing the nutrients, acids and sugar. Add 100 p.p.m. sulphite (2 Campden tablets) and introduce the yeast 24 hours later. Ferment on the pulp for three days then strain it off and press lightly. Add the grape concentrate and elderflowers and ferment on the latter for a further 2–3 days. Make the volume up to 4.5 litres (1 gal.) with water and allow to ferment to dryness. Thereafter proceed as instructed in the basic procedure.

## RECIPE 5

*Ingredients:*

1.8 kg (4 lb.) cherries
450 g (1 lb.) sultanas
280 ml (½ pt.) red rose petals
Nutrients
Burgundy yeast
675 g (1½ lb.) clover honey
Water to 4.5 litres (1 gal.)

*Method:*

Crush the cherries, taking care not to break any stones, add the washed sultanas and 3 litres (5 pt.) water containing the honey and nutrients. Add 100 p.p.m. sulphite (2 Campden tablets) and introduce the yeast starter after 24 hours. Ferment on the pulp for three days then strain it off and press lightly. After another four days, add the rose petals and ferment on the flowers for two-three days. Make the volume up to 4.5 litres (1 gal.) with cold water and ferment to dryness. Thereafter continue as directed in the basic procedure.

**RECIPE 6 (25 litres (5 gal.))**

*Ingredients:*

   1.3 kg (3 lb.) dried apricots
   450 g (1 lb.) dried elderberries
   900 g (2 lb.) raspberries
   1.1 litres (2 pt.) white grape concentrate
   Rhône or Burgundy yeast
   1.1 litres (2 pt.) rose petals (mixed red and yellow)
   Nutrients
   2.7 kg (6 lb.) sugar
   Water to 25 litres (5 gal.)

*Method:*

Wash the apricots and elderberries and mix with the crushed raspberries. Add 18 litres (4 gal.) cold water containing the sugar nutrients and 100 p.p.m. sulphite (10 Campden tablets – 2 per 4.5 litres (1 gal.)) After 24 hours introduce the yeast and ferment on the pulp for two-three days before straining it off and pressing lightly. Add the grape concentrate and about four days later add the rose petals. Ferment on the flowers for two-three days, then strain them off and make the volume up to 25 litres (5 gal.) with water. Ferment until the gravity drops to 0, rack and add 50 p.p.m. sulphite (1 Campden tablet per 4.5 litres (1 gal.)). Rack again as soon as fermentation restarts or a heavy deposit is formed, whichever is the sooner. Thereafter continue as directed in the basic procedure.

# CHAPTER X

# Champagne

A great many amateur winemakers in this country make Champagne-type wines with great success and safety. It is nevertheless necessary to issue a preliminary warning that this is not a beginner's wine. Great pressure exists inside Champagne bottles, as great or greater than the pressure in a car tyre, and accidents do occur occasionally in even commercial Champagne making.

This can be illustrated by relating what befell a man who used to live in the Old Kent Road area of London close to the Elephant and Castle. He did everything on a grandiose scale. When wishing to put a nail in a door to hang coats on, he would use a six-inch nail so that coats could be hung on both sides of the door. He had a grape-vine growing dustily outside his backdoor and one day he announced to his neighbours that he was "going to 'ave a bash" at making Champagne. He sent his children scurrying hither and thither for bottles, yeast, sugar etc. and soon had a ferment going, which, after a couple of days fermentation he filtered and bottled. In his grandiose manner he acquired some outsize corks which he hammered into bottles and then retired to bed well-satisfied with his achievements. During the night the corks shot the ceiling down, and when the winemaker came scampering down the stairs and stood amid the damp plaster debris he said with emphasis "You can't make wine from English grapes!"

Had he wired on the corks the bottles would have burst, and it is this latter danger that made us hesitate a little before writing this Champagne article.

There are several different methods of making Champagne-type wines. The one outlined here has stood the test of time, and has been used by amateur winemakers all over the country with a minimum risk of breakages. Some of the wines produced by this method are certainly up to the standard of the cheaper Champagnes of commerce, although none of them can of course hope to match the brilliance of quality that is experienced in Vintage Champagne.

Whether it is an actual fact with scientific reasons or merely a conditioning of our minds, Champagne seems to have a different effect on the drinker from that of other wines. The bubbling effervescence of the wine seems to transmit its joy to the drinker, and people become light-hearted and even romantic. Under the influence of Champagne old people feel a temporary return of the vitality and joie-de-vivre of their youth.

Sparkling wines have been made for centuries all over the world, and many readers will be familiar with the Italian wine Asti Spumante, the Portuguese Mateus Rosé, Sparkling Anjou from the Loire, and Sparkling White Burgundy. In earlier days ingenious methods were used to trap the bubbles of carbon dioxide, and special stout-walled casks were used, bunged down tight.

It is probable that sparkling wines were made more or less accidentally at first. In the past, wines were generally drunk soon after fermentation, within months, since otherwise with their low alcoholic content, and poor methods of storage, they would not keep. In some years, however, when the sun shone hot and long the increased sugar content of the grapes resulted in a stronger wine which could be stored well into the following year. It was discovered that these wines not infrequently became sparkling and effervesced when opened. History written at the time records that this was due to a second fermentation occurring in the bottle when the warmer weather returned. To some extent this is true, but the high malic acid content of the grapes in the Northern vineyards leads one to suspect that a malo-lactic "fermentation" was also partly responsible. Many winemakers will have experienced this occasionally when opening a bottle of wine that was perfectly stable when bottled.

The great genius in Champagne making was a Benedictine monk named Dom Perignon, who was as far ahead of his time scientifically in the wine world as was Leonardo da Vinci in his sphere. The methods he introduced, following his appointment as cellarer to the Abbey of Haut-Villiers in the Champagne district of France, were so good that even today only minor improvements have been made.

The obvious scientific invention he made was to use the bark of the cork-oak to effectively seal bottles. This invention has of course affected the entire wine world since corks have become the standard method of sealing bottles. Another invention of his, less obvious, but more significant, from the point of view of Champagne, was the development of a blending system which is the basis of the present-day cuvée method, which is mainly responsible for the gradual emergence of Champagne as the outstanding sparkling wine, head and shoulders above every other type of sparkling wine.

We are talking here of the best Champagnes, of course, for the poorer Champagnes can sometimes be surpassed by the sparkling wines of other regions of France or other countries. There are so many factors involved in Champagne making that the chances of error are greater than in the other wines. As a result, Champagne is either superb or poor, but rarely mediocre. The poorer Champagnes are the ones which we buy at around £3 a bottle for parties in order to liven things up rapidly. The superb Champagnes are well over twice the price, and are eagerly sought by connoisseurs, and drunk as they should be as a table wine right through the meal.

There are three main methods of producing wines of the Champagne type. The principal one of these, for producing large quantities of cheap Champagne, is by tank fermentation. This is not of value to the amateur winemaker since we do not have at our disposal the means with which to emulate it.

The second method is by artificially impregnating a stable still wine with carbon dioxide. This procedure produces moderately good results provided the basic wine is a good one. The wine, ready matured and cleared, is drawn off into Champagne bottles, dosed with spirit or brandy, and impregnated with $CO_2$ by means of a special machine. Facilities for amateurs to do this are comparatively limited, and in practice it is hardly worthwhile although some successful methods have been published.

The 'bubbly' bottle on the market today, will produce a poor mans 'champagne' in a minute! Fill about ¾ full with a chilled white wine. Insert the bottle, and charge with $CO_2$ till the pressure release valve blows. Unscrew your gas bottle, release the pressure in the bottle and then remove cap and pour out a litre of instant champagne.

**The only really practicable method for the amateur is the original, well-proved one of bottle fermentation. This genuine French method, laborious though it may be, always gives the best Champagne in the end.**

First let us look at the way the French do it. Only the choicest grapes are used and great care is taken that no mouldy or unripe grapes are included. These grapes are then directly pressed, without any prior treatment or pulp fermentation, and this juice, known as the Cuvée, forms the basis of this superb wine beloved of connoisseurs.

The juice is lightly sulphited and then is impregnated with a Champagne yeast culture and fermented in vats for up to eight weeks in a fairly cool temperature.

After 8–10 weeks the wine is racked and is then blended with the products of other vintages. This blending is of vital importance in order to even out the variations caused by climate, soil, etc., so as to produce a finished wine of constant high quality.

A little later, the wine is carefully filtered to remove all cloudy matter, and is then dosed with sugar syrup and a special Champagne yeast. The amount of sugar required to be added is of vital importance in order to obtain the correct pressure of carbon dioxide inside the bottle.

**It has been found that 16 grammes of sugar to each litre of wine will give a gas pressure of 4 atmospheres (55 lbs. per square inch), and that has been found to be best in practice. In amateur winemaking terms this represents 70–85 g (2½–3 oz.) sugar per 4.5 litres (1 gal.), or 15 g (½ oz.) per bottle.**

Some leading amateur winemakers tend to use a little less than this, but it would seem that this is a satisfactory as well as safe quantity to add.

**The addition of further sugar is to be avoided, for the pressure can then easily rise to greater pressures than the bottles can withstand. Champagne bottles, when new, are said to be able to withstand 8 atmospheres pressure, but once used, and having collected a series of outside scratches, they are greatly weakened thereby so that it is necessary to err on the side of safety.**

The wine, now dosed with sugar syrup and yeast, is drawn off into thick glass bottles, filled to within 2½ inches of the rim, and stoppered with good quality corks which are carefully wired down.

The bottles are then laid at a slight angle in special racks called pupitres ("desks") and the temperature is maintained at 18° C (65°F) so that the desired bottle fermentation gets under way. After a couple of weeks the temperature is lowered to 10°C (50°F) so as to avoid a build up of excessive pressure in the bottles. The wine is now left for 1–3 years to mature; according to quality, during which time the wine is in contact with the yeast. The minimum period of one year is legally enforced in France.

For the first two months the bottles are given a slight twist each day and the bottle is gradually angled more and more so that eventually it is standing on its head. This process, known as Rémuage, is carried out in order to bring the yeast sediment down on to the cork, leaving the Champagne clear above it.

At this point, the mass of yeast settled on the cork has to be removed, a process known as dégorgement. So that this can be done without disturbance of the sediment or loss of gas, the bottles are first chilled and then the wiring is removed, the cork shoots out and the bottles are turned upright and lightly corked. When a series of bottles have been treated in this way each bottle receives a dose of brandy or brandy and syrup depending on the required sweetness of the finished Champagne, after which they are again well corked down and wired, leaving an air space of about 20 mm (¾ in.) between the wine and the bottom of the cork.

Another method of dégorgement in use is to employ a freezing bath held at the temperature of −20°C (−4°F) by means of which the wine in the neck of the bottle is frozen and an ice-plug of frozen wine and yeast sediment is ejected with the cork.

# Method for Amateur Winemakers

It is not too difficult to adapt the commercial method to amateur winemakers' needs. It is, however, necessary to impress on readers that champagne making cannot be done casually. The work is a labour of love, and this can only be achieved when one becomes dedicated to champagne making as a hobby in its own right, and not just as a means to an end.

We would not ourselves attempt to make champagne without the aid of a hydrometer and some sugar testing kit such as the Clinitest. In the following two methods described, the use of these aids is mentioned alongside the general instructions.

## METHOD 1

(a) Prepare the must in the usual way as per recipe and introduce a yeast starter. It is important that not more than 450 g (1 lb.) of sugar per 4.5 litres (1 gal.) be used in addition to the fruit, unless a hydrometer be used, in which case a starting gravity of 60–65 is desirable. All the sugar is added at the start of fermentation.

(b) The yeast used should be a genuine Champagne yeast such as Grey Owl Champagne, Vierka Perlschaum, Kitzinger Champagne or Vinotex Champagne (other Champagne yeasts are probably suitable but have been omitted merely because we have not ourselves tried them).

(c) Allow the wine to ferment in the usual manner, but rack it off its yeast as soon as the first tumultuous fermentation has subsided (this will occur approximately when the hydrometer reading is 5 and ideally when a sugar test shows that $1\frac{1}{2}$ per cent to $1\frac{3}{4}$ per cent sugar is remaining).

(d) The wine now starting its secondary fermentation is bottled in champagne bottles with special champagne corks bound on crosswise.

(e) The bottles are kept for eight days in a warm room (between 17°C (65°F) and 20°C (70°F)) and are then moved to a cooler place (around 12°C (50°F)).

(f) The bottles should be stored (preferably for six months at least) on a slight incline, cork downwards, and each day for a week or so each bottle must be given an abrupt jerk an eighth of a turn to left and right.

(g) After at least a week of the "rémuage" it will be found that the yeast sediment has settled on the cork, and a further wait is necessary merely to allow the wine to become thoroughly clear above. Cautious winemakers use a piece of blanket to hold the base of the bottle while carrying out this operation, in case a weakened bottle has been used.

(h) When the wine is clear, the yeast sediment must be removed. This is a job requiring great care and some skill. The bottle is held at a steep angle, neck downwards with one hand supporting it from beneath, while the other hand removes the fastening and carefully eases out the cork. It will slide out slowly at first and then suddenly shoot out carrying the yeast with it. Immediately the bottle must be turned upright and a thumb placed on top to force the carbon dioxide effervescence to die down. The last traces of yeast are then removed from the neck of the bottle with a finger and a small glass of brandy or brandy plus sugar syrup is added according to taste. The bottle is then restoppered and again fastened with stout string or wire.

The actual dosage should be all brandy if a very dry champagne is required or all sugar syrup if a sweet champagne is desired. Once you have made your first batch you will quickly decide when drinking it whether to use the same dosage on future occasions or whether to make a mixture of brandy and sugar syrup.

(i) The process can be made easier by employing a freezing bath of ice cubes and ordinary common salt, into which the necks of the bottles are placed for a while until a pellet of ice is seen to form in the neck of the bottle. This pellet of ice is forced out with the cork and less wine is lost than in the method described above. The sediment is also prevented from being disturbed during these operations because it is enclosed within the plug of ice in the neck of the bottle.

(j) The bottles are then stored on their sides in a cool temperature for about a year before drinking.

Yet another method of removing the unwanted yeast is the Southern Vineyard Vinetrap. This is a special blister cork which collects the dead yeast whilst the bottle is inverted. Once the Champagne is clear, the blister is wired off. The bottle chilled in a refrigerator. The gas dissolves in the wine, the Vintrap is removed and replaced by a plastic Champagne cork.

## METHOD 2

This involves making a champagne from a completely finished wine. The two points to observe here are:-

(a) the wine must not be above 8% alcohol (which again means a starting gravity of about 60).

(b) It must be perfectly clear (to achieve this quickly it is essential to have a balanced must and in some cases to use pectinol or other pectin-destroying enzyme in the must).

The cleared wine is drawn off into champagne bottles (ordinary ones may not be used as they cannot withstand the pressure) and a small glass of yeast culture is added. This has been prepared beforehand and is in full ferment when added.

The actual wine should be tested beforehand with a sugar testing kit (which should give a reading of ¼ per cent or ½ per cent sugar only).

The wine can then be primed with sugar syrup before putting in bottles and refermenting. For exact measurements the following table will be of use. It should be remembered that the Clinitest sugar testing kit will only measure invert sugar, and while any original sugar added at the start of fermentation would have become invert sugar in the presence of yeast and acids, these kits will not measure very recently added sugar which has not yet been inverted.

To obtain about four atmospheres pressure we require 1½% sugar which is 15–16 grams per litre or 70 grams per gallon.

| Sugar remaining in wine | Sugar to be added per 4.5 litres (1 gal.) before bottling |
|---|---|
| 0 | 70 g (2½ oz.) per 4.5 litres (1 gal.) |
| ¼% | 60 g (2¼ oz.) per 4.5 litres (1 gal.) |
| ½% | 50 g (1¾ oz.) per 4.5 litres (1 gal.) |
| ¾% | 40 g (1½ oz.) per 4.5 litres (1 gal.) |
| 1 % | 25 g (1 oz.) per 4.5 litres (1 gal.) |
| 1¼% | 15 g ( ½ oz.) per 4.5 litres (1 gal.) |
| 1½% | 5 g ( ¼ oz.) per 4.5 litres (1 gal.) |
| 1¾% | Nil |

Wines containing 2% or more sugar should not be used for champagne production.

The bottles are dealt with in exactly the same way as in Method 1 (from point (e) onwards).

Before continuing with some recipes, let us reiterate the safety precautions required:

**1. Never make champagne without using a hydrometer and a sugar testing kit.**

2. Not more than 450 g (1 lb.) of sugar per 4.5 litres (1 gal.) in addition to that in the fruit (starting gravity of 60).

3. Use champagne bottles.

4. When handling bottles hold them in a piece of thick blanket and keep your face away from the bottles as far as possible.

## RECIPE 1

*Ingredients:*

> 1.8 kg (4 lb.) green gooseberries
> 280 ml (½ pt.) white grape concentrate
> 280 ml (½ pt.) elderflowers or yellow rose petals (lightly pressed down only)
> 15 g (½ oz.) pectinol
> Yeast nutrient
> Champagne yeast
> Honey or sugar syrup to gravity 60
> Water to 4.5 litres (1 gal.)

*Method:*

Place the gooseberries in a plastic bucket and bruise them well with a piece of wood. Add the flowers and pour over them 3 litres (6½ pt.) of boiling water. When cool add the grape concentrate, yeast nutrient and pectinol and enough sugar syrup or honey syrup to produce a gravity of 60

Add the yeast starter and ferment on the pulp for three days, after which strain off the fermenting must from the pulp and continue fermentation in a glass jar under fermentation lock. Then proceed as detailed in either Method 1 or 2.

## RECIPE 2

*Ingredients:*

> 450 g (1 lb.) dried apricots
> 280 ml (½ pt.) white grape concentrate
> 280 ml (½ pt.) elderflowers or yellow rose petals
> 15 g (½ oz.) malic acid
> Yeast nutrient
> 10 g (¼ oz.) pectinol
> Water to 4.5 litres (1 gal.)
> Honey or sugar syrup to gravity 60

*Method:*

Place the apricots and flowers in a plastic bucket and pour 3 litres (6½ pt.) boiling water over them. When cool add the malic acid, yeast nutrient and pectinol, stir well and adjust the gravity to 60 with sugar syrup or honey.

Add the yeast starter and ferment on the pulp for 2–3 days only, after which strain off into a demijohn and continue fermentation. Then proceed as described in Method 1 or 2.

## RECIPE 3

*Ingredients:*

> **4.5 litres (1 gal.) pear juice or 2.25 litres (½ gal.) each, pear and dessert apple juice**
> **280 ml (½ pt.) white grape concentrate**
> **280 ml (½ pt.) elderflowers or yellow rose petals**
> **10 g (¼ oz.) pectinol**
> **Yeast nutrients**
> **Champagne yeast**

*Method:*

Place all the ingredients in a plastic bucket and stir well until thoroughly mixed. Adjust the gravity to 60 with sugar if too low or with water if too high and add an active yeast starter. When fermentation is going well transfer to a jar. Then proceed as detailed in Method 1 or 2.

# Other Sparkling Wines

## RECIPE 4

*Ingredients*

> **450 g (1 lb.) elderberries**
> **450 g (1 lb.) raisins**
> **15 g (½ oz.) malic acid**
> **Yeast nutrient**
> **10 g (¼ oz.) pectinol**
> **Water to 4.5 litres (1 gal.)**
> **Sugar syrup to gravity 60**

116

*Method*

Placed chopped raisins and crushed elderberries in a plastic bucket and pour 3 litres (6½ pt.) boiling water over them. When cool add the malic acid, yeast nutrient and pectinol. Stir well and adjust the gravity to 60 with sugar syrup.

Add the yeast starter (Champagne, Burgundy or Bordeaux) and ferment on the pulp for 3 days, after which strain off into a demijohn jar and continue fermenting. Then proceed as described in Method 1 or 2.

## RECIPE 5

*Ingredients*

**225 g (½ lb.) dried bilberries**
**280 ml (½ pt.) white grape concentrate**
**15 g (½ oz.) malic acid**
**Yeast nutrient**
**10 g (¼ oz.) pectinol**
**Water to 4.5 litres (1 gal.)**
**Honey or sugar syrup to gravity 60**

*Method*

Place the bilberries and grape concentrate in a plastic bucket and pour 3 litres (6½ pt.) boiling water over them. When cool add the malic acid, yeast nutrient and pectinol. Stir well and adjust the gravity to 60 with honey or sugar syrup. Add an active Burgundy yeast starter and ferment on the pulp for 4–5 days until a sufficient depth of colour has been achieved, after which strain off into a demijohn jar and continue fermentation. Then continue as in Method 1 or 2.

# CHAPTER XI

# Liqueurs and Aperitifs

What is a Liqueur? ... The basic definition is that it is a sweetened and flavoured alcoholic beverage obtained by the distillation or infusion of aromatic and/or fruit substances with potable spirit. The very name "Liqueur" conjures up notions of lush banquets just finishing with diners groaning contentedly over their Cointreau, or the lounge bars of fashionable London taverns where Green Chartreuse is sipped in oddly shaped glasses with one's little finger cocked. In actual fact Liqueurs have become so muddled with other drinks, that it seems best to lump them all together at the start and sort them out as we go, alphabetically.

In most wine catalogues Aperitifs and Liqueurs will occupy different sections, and in some catalogues other titles also appear, such as: Fruit Brandies, Cups and Bitters, Alcoholic Cordials. Further confusion arises when such drinks as the familiar Egg Flip (Advocaat) are found in the Aperitif section of one catalogue and in the Liqueur section of another. Pernod, the fiery heir of the now banned Absinthe, is an aperitif, but in view of its considerable alcoholic strength it is often bought and drunk by many people as though it were a liqueur even though it lacks the sweetness that is normal in a liqueur.

However, sweet or dry, whether drunk before or after meals, or in one's bath, the fact emerges that liqueurs can be made very simply by any amateur winemaker. It is just a matter of obtaining the correct flavouring essence (all sorts of which are now readily available), using a reasonably or even a poor home-made wine as a base to supply part of the alcohol, adding sugar syrup and a spirit, and you are there. In most cases the liqueur or aperitif is ready for immediate drinking. At this point, however, let us issue a note of warning, just to clear the air:

**Home-made liqueurs and aperitifs must not be sold. Also, some liqueurs such as Benedictine, Chartreuse, Grand Marnier and**

118

*"A chirping cup is my matin song . . ."*
Liqueurs were the creation in the main of monasteries, but they
enjoyed other forms of refreshment too!

**Strega are proprietary names and in consequence home-made liqueurs should not be labelled with these names.**

In the recipes that follow it is not claimed that any of these will produce a product which is identical to the liqueurs described in the heading above the recipe.

Digressing for a moment, it is curious how "touchy" some makers of drinks are about any attempt on the part of the amateur to copy their products, even though no question of selling them is involved. There was a certain amount of prejudice against amateurs in the early days of the winemaking movement. Voices were even raised within the movement against the establishment of a National Committee lest this centralisation should invite legislation against us in Parliament, pressurised by the big commercial concerns.

In actual fact, the large wine companies such as Grants of St. James, the Victoria Wine Company and Harveys of Bristol have gone out of their way to be pleasant and friendly to amateur winemakers, giving lectures with splendid free samples. They knew what they were doing, for during the period 1958–1963 when the amateur winemaking movement was mushrooming, clearances of wine through Customs in Britain rose from 15 million gallons to 23 million gallons. This is an average increase of 10% per annum, considerably in excess of the 4% rise in productivity desired by the rest of the country's industries.

The truth of the matter is that if you make a wine or a liqueur that should bear some resemblance to a commercial article, you cannot resist nipping round to the off-licence to buy a bottle of the real thing to see how well you have triumphed in your own efforts.

If liqueur making becomes popular in amateur circles the sales of liqueurs will boom as have the wine sales. It's not just what you drink yourself – for if you have something good you let your friends taste it and they will acquire the taste for it, and so the gentle art of gracious tippling spreads throughout the whole community.

# Fascinating Variety

You have to experience the vast range of flavours that exist in the world of liqueurs and aperitifs to appreciate what a fascinating territory exists for your exploring. One of the authors has (or rather had) a fair-sized collection of miniatures gathered from all over Europe. Miniatures seem to be a recognised form of present at Christmas and for birthdays to give amateur wine-makers. Their attractive shapes and colours add an air of quality to the multitude of tiny bars that we possess in our wineries.

Not so long ago, on an impulse, with a few friends, it was decided to liquidate this collection and a most exciting exploration of this scintillating world of liqueurs took place over several evenings. The bottles still stand on the shelves above the bar, now alas filled with Apricot wine only, but their memory lives on as one's glance wanders from bottle to bottle.

# The Flavouring

In the course of preparing this section, it was necessary to check on most of the recipes issued by the manufacturing companies supplying the essences. Indeed, in some cases four or five checks on the one recipe were made with different wines, strengths of spirit and even different base spirits.

It would have taken the resources of a Rothschild to have made a complete bottle for each experiment and thus a laboratory method of preparing small samples had to be devised.

After a few initial failures this technique proved so successful that it is possible, armed with a variety of essences, one or two bottles of basic wine, some sugar syrup and half a bottle of Polish spirit to make glasses of liqueurs to order, so to speak. This laboratory method will be outlined in detail in a later section, as it may prove of value to wine guilds seeking their own individual guild liqueur without spending too much of the guild funds in the search for the right recipe.

**Extracts are supplied by T. Noirot Extracts and flavours and essences by Vina and other winemakers' suppliers.**

We must admit that our recipes differ considerably in some cases from those advocated by the supplier of the essence. This is a case of our personal taste. We must also add that for some types of liqueurs one supplier's essence was found to be greatly superior to another's. This too may be a question of personal taste. In the long run quality will triumph, so, if you find that a liqueur is not quite up to your expectations, first try an alternative essence if one is available, and if that is still not successful, change your basic wine. In many cases the change of essence will achieve the success you require.


## Essences Intended to Improve Wines

Essence-bottle browsing at your local supplier can become as fascinating a pastime as the Charing Cross Road is to book-lovers. In the course of browsing you will come across a wide variety, including Sherry, Port, Madeira, Burgundy, Gin, Whisky and Brandy (or Eau-de-vie). Strictly speaking these are intended for improving poor flavoured wines. The idea is that you make a wheat wine, say, add a little of the whisky extract and give the wine to your friends hoping they will think you have a secret still.

The gin flavours seem to have greatest possibilities, we feel. There are still many unsolved problems in winemaking, and one of these is what to do with friends who are confirmed spirit drinkers. Now most gin drinkers do not drink it neat, but generally with water or bitter lemon. This dilution brings the strength down to about 35° proof. It should therefore be possible to make a wine of a fairly neutral and almost colourless nature, add to it some gin essence and possibly some citron essence, fortify it slightly by about 3 fluid ounces of 140° proof spirit per bottle and give it to friends who will think they are drinking gin and bitter lemon. The difficulty is finding the right ingredients, and so far we have not ourselves found the answer.

The whisky flavour is also a difficult one to match and would require a grain wine base. Rum however offers a much greater chance of success since many people (other than Naval diehards) tend to drink it with orange. If you have some Seville Orange wine that still has a little "bite" to it try adding a little rum flavour to it – an interesting drink to end an evening.

But this is a digression; let us return to our liqueurs proper …

Southern Vinyards have introduced 3 speciality concentrates – Ginora, Whiskora and Brandora, fermented in the normal way as kit concentrates. By adding a bottle of your favourite commercial spirit you will end up with seven bottles at roughly a quarter of the price of commercial equivalents.

# The Basic Wine

Since most liqueurs and aperitifs range in strength from about 30° proof up to lone giants such as Green Chartreuse (96° proof) it is important that a strong wine is used as a base.

We have assumed in these recipes that a wine of 28° proof is available (this is 16% alcohol by volume and equals the strength of our strong wines). What is more important is that the wine should normally not have too powerful a flavour of its own. There are nevertheless exceptions to this rule, for in the course of one experiment it was found that a powerfully flavoured Elderberry wine blended wonderfully with an orange essence to produce a new flavour which was neither elderberry nor orange.

By and large, however, rather dull uninteresting wines seem to be more suitable and their main function in these cases is simply to provide part of the required alcohol. The question of the colour of the wine is not important except for the purists. Liqueurs are as individual as their makers in the commercial field, and such liqueurs as Curacao appear in red, white and even blue colours. The familiar Creme-de-Menthe is best known in its green form but white and pink varieties also exist.

# The Spirit

For most purposes, 140° proof Polish spirit is the best medium for fortification, since it is neutral in taste and so strong that it is well above the strength of the most powerful liqueurs (which in general range around 70° proof, the strength of whisky, gin rum and brandy). Certain of the lower strength liqueurs and fruit brandies in the range 35–50° proof can be made with advantage with brandy, rum or gin, but we suggest some initial experimentation with small quantities as described in the next section before full-scale production is attempted. It is unfortunate that the customs duty on Polish spirit raises its price to £9.50 approximately per half bottle, but half a bottle goes a long way, especially with the lower strength liqueurs such as Cherry Brandy.

# The Syrup

The sweetening syrup is made by heating 900 g (2 lb.) of sugar with 570 ml (1 pt.) of water, allowing it to boil for a few moments until the solution becomes quite clear and colourless. This syrup must, of course, be allowed to cool before being used.

The basic method of preparing liqueurs and aperitifs is very simple. Take an ordinary kitchen measure, measure the amount of Polish spirit required, add the essence, mix well and pour into the bottle. Then measure the amount of syrup required and pour this into the bottle. Pour a little wine into the measure, swirling it round to wash the last traces of the spirit, essence and syrup and add it to the bottle. Finally top up the bottle with more wine. The bottle should then be well shaken to mix the ingredients. The kitchen measure should not be washed between additions, for it is essential that all traces of the essence eventually finish up in the bottle, most being added with the spirit but traces with the syrup and wine.

Most liqueurs are ready to drink immediately after mixing, since they do not mature with age as do wines. The essential factor to ensure success is that all the ingredients should become intimately mixed. Only with the more delicately flavoured liqueurs is there a slight advantage in leaving the liqueurs to stand for a week or two or even a month or so.

## Procedure

The following table gives the relative amounts in millilitres which will produce sample lots of 80 ml of liqueurs of various strengths. Since 80 ml is approximately one tenth of a bottle it is ample to allow four or five people to taste each liqueur sample.

| Wine 28° Proof | Sugar Syrup | Spirit 140° Proof | Final strength of liqueur |
|---|---|---|---|
| 56 ml | 15 ml | 9 ml | 35° Proof |
| 53 ml | 15 ml | 12 ml | 40° Proof |
| 50 ml | 15 ml | 15 ml | 44° Proof |
| 47 ml | 15 ml | 18 ml | 48° Proof |
| 44 ml | 15 ml | 21 ml | 52° Proof |
| 41 ml | 15 ml | 24 ml | 56° Proof |
| 38 ml | 15 ml | 27 ml | 60° Proof |
| 35 ml | 15 ml | 30 ml | 64° Proof |
| 32 ml | 15 ml | 33 ml | 69° Proof |
| 29 ml | 15 ml | 36 ml | 73° Proof |
| 26 ml | 15 ml | 39 ml | 77° Proof |

In the lower strength liqueurs (say 44° Proof) a half bottle of 140° Polish spirit will serve for over 20 separate experiments with four or five people tasting each time, (a half bottle contains just under 400 ml).

We have maintained the syrup level as a constant in the above table but this can be varied as explained later.

There are only two simple pieces of equipment required. One is a graduated one millilitre pipette (eye-dropper type) and the other is a 100 ml measuring cylinder. These two items cost only a few pence each at most chemists or specialist shops.

## Test Sampling

The initial part of each test tasting is very simple. Let us suppose that the tasting committee decide that for a start they are thinking in terms of a liqueur of about 56° proof strength. Wine is first poured into the measuring cylinder up to the 41 ml mark (see table). Then 15 ml of sugar syrup are poured in, bringing it up to the 56 ml mark. Then 24 ml Polish spirit (140° Proof) are poured in as indicated by the table bringing the level up to the 80 ml mark. All that has to be done now is to introduce the extract or essence, stir well and drink.

The introduction of the flavourings needs a steady hand and a clear mind. There is nearly always someone with these qualities in every guild who is capable of handling a 1 ml graduated pipette accurately. The essences themselves are supplied in varying strengths according to manufacturer. Since in these test samples we are making only one tenth of a bottle of liqueur at a time, it is necessary to use only one tenth the amount of extract. A teaspoon holds 3 ml, so that wherever one teaspoonful of essence is mentioned in a recipe, only 0.3 ml (three tenths of a millilitre) are required in these test samples. It is very much simpler to do than to describe. If however, difficulty is experienced in obtaining three tenths of a millilitre, or if a graduated 1 ml pipette is not easily obtainable, the ordinary 1 ml pipette (which has just the single 1 ml mark on it) can be used. Simply pour wine into the measuring cylinder up to the 30 ml mark, add the 1 ml of essence and stir well. Then pour off 20 ml of this into some other container, and the 10 ml remaining will contain the one teaspoonful equivalent of essence per bottle. The wine is then made up to its original mark according to the table.

From these test samplings a very good idea can be obtained of how the extracts blend with the different types of wine and it can be decided whether the sugar level is too high or low.

Once a satisfactory formula has been discovered and all the tasting committee sworn to secrecy, a full bottle can be made with accuracy.

# Strength

Sometimes the tasting committee will deviate from the preceding table, and arrive at a satisfactory formula but not any longer be able to define the strength of the liqueur. This is easily arrived at in the following manner. Let us suppose that 20 ml wine, 10 ml sugar syrup and 20 ml spirit produced the final liqueur. Simply multiply each item by its alcohol strength (including the sugar which has a Nil strength) and divide by the total volume.

| Volume multiplied by Strength | | | | Total |
|---|---|---|---|---|
| Wine | 20 ml | x | 28° | 560 |
| Sugar | 10 | x | Nil | 0 |
| Spirit | 20 | x | 140° | 2800 |
| | Total 50 ml | | | 3360 |

Divide the 3360 by 50 and the answer is 67° proof.

If the same proportions were used but the wine was only 25° proof and ordinary gin (70° proof) was being used the figures would be:

| | | | | |
|---|---|---|---|---|
| Wine | 20 ml | x | 25° proof equals | 500 |
| Sugar | 10 | x | Nil | 0 |
| Gin | 20 | x | 70° | 1400 |
| | Total 50 ml | | | 1900 |

1900 divided by 50 gives 38° proof strength of liqueur.

After that mathematical orgy it is as well to return to recipes. All recipes are for one full wine-bottle of liqueur.

# Absinthe Group

These are Spirit Aperitifs, but the French drink them at all times of day and night. **Absinthe** itself, a popular bit of still-life in French Impressionist painting, is now banned because of its ill-effects on health when drunk in quantity. Its heirs, **Pernod, Pastis, Anice, Anise, Anesone,** and **Anisette** do not have the stigma of Absinthe. Indeed, if one has indigestion or mild stomach upsets it is difficult to find a better cure than three glasses of Pernod sipped steadily over the course of an evening. The following recipes have a similar flavouring base.

## RECIPE 1

*Ingredients:*

**340 ml (13 fl. oz.) of 140° proof spirit**
**150 ml (5 fl. oz.) of sugar syrup**
**One teaspoonful Vina Anise essence**
**Top up bottle with white wine of low flavour**
**This aperitif will be 77° proof strength**

## RECIPE 2

**360 ml (12 fl. oz.) of 140° Polish spirit**
**150 ml (5 fl. oz.) of sugar syrup**
**2 teaspoonfuls T. Noirot Anisette extract**
**Top up bottle with white wine**
**This aperitif will be of 73° proof strength**

A slightly drier aperitif can be made using only 90 ml (3 fl. oz.) of sugar syrup, and in this case only one teaspoonful of essence is normally required.

## RECIPE 3

**330 ml (11 fl. oz.) of 140° Polish spirit**
**120 ml (4 fl. oz.) sugar syrup**
**1 teaspoonful Vina Anisette essence**
**Top up bottle with white wine**
**This aperitif will be 70° proof strength**

During the war, the one spirit forbidden to the troops was Arack (also known as Araq, Ouzo and about two hundred other local names, including a few by courtesy of the British Army). It was said to be bad for their health, but after a dozen forbidden Aracks it was generally the local population whose health tended to be put in jeopardy by the belligerence engendered by this fiery spirit. Modern Arack on sale in this country is a refined thing rated as magnificent by many people. The following recipes tend to approach the real thing and are certainly far superior to the local-made stuff retailed by oasis Arabs or the primitive tribes of the former East Indies.

## RECIPE 4

**360 ml (12 fl. oz.) 140° proof spirit**
**150 ml (5 fl. oz.) sugar spirit**
**150 ml (5 fl. oz.) whisky**
**2 teaspoonfuls T. Noirot Anisette extract**
**Top up with white wine (a grain wine for preference)**
**This is 83° proof strength**

## RECIPE 5

**360 ml (12 fl. oz.) 140° proof spirit**
**150 ml (5 fl. oz.) sugar syrup**
**1 teaspoonful Vina Anise essence**
**Top up with Irish Whiskey**

This powerful concoction of 86° proof strength needs to be treated with considerable respect.

# Advocaat

In wine merchants' catalogues they seem to call it Advocaat in the liqueur section and Egg Flip in the cocktail section. In the Army it was called Egg Nog and we are indebted to Bill Gregory for the following recipe which he has made in the Warrant Officers' Messes of Austria, Burma and elsewhere in the Orient. It is an excellent pick-me-up for invalids and said to be beloved by duchesses.

*Ingredients:*

**The yolks of 3 large eggs**
**120 ml (4 fl. oz.) of sugar syrup**
**180 ml (6 fl. oz.) of gin or brandy**
**Vanilla essence to taste**
**Evaporated milk as required**

128

*Method:*

Chill all the ingredients in the refrigerator if possible. Beat the egg yolks well, and then add the sugar syrup, gin or brandy and a little of the evaporated milk (say 120 ml (4 fl. oz.)). Continue beating until all are well blended. The ideal consistency of this liqueur is that it should only just pour, and enough additional evaporated milk should be beaten in to achieve this consistency. The amount required largely depends on the size of the eggs used. Finally add the vanilla essence to taste.


# Apricot Brandy

We have always been scrupulously honest with our readers, never pandering to popular appeal or covering up our differences or failures, and we must admit here that we ran into difficulties when first making test liqueurs of the Apricot Brandy type. It seems to us that Apricot wine would make an excellent base for Apricot Brandy, but apparently this is not necessarily so, and a "scruffy" old Banana wine proved a much better base.


## RECIPE 1

*Ingredients:*

**240 ml (8 fl. oz.) 140° proof spirit**
**150 ml (5 fl. oz.) of sugar syrup**
**2 teaspoonfuls T. Noirot Apricot Brandy extract**
**Top up with a white wine**
**This is 56° proof strength**


## RECIPE 2

**270 ml (9 fl. oz.) 140° proof spirit**
**240 ml ( 8 fl. oz.) sugar syrup**
**2 teaspoonfuls T. Noirot Apricot Brandy extract**
**Top up with white wine**
**This is 57° proof strength and represents the sweeter version of
   Apricot Brandy**

## RECIPE 3

210 ml (7 fl. oz.) 140° proof spirit
90 ml (3 fl. oz.) sugar syrup
1 teaspoonful Vina Apricot Brandy essence
Top up with white wine
This is 54° proof strength, and is much drier than the other versions. It can in fact be used as an aperitif

# Benedictine

This magnificent herb-based liqueur, another great product of the Benedictine monks, is very well known. The familiar bottles bear the letters D.O.M. which stands for "Deo Optimo Maximo" – "To God, the Most Good, the Most Great," a motto worthy of Benedictine since it is probably one of the oldest of liqueurs, being made originally at the now ruined Abbey of Fécamp, in Normandy.

It is one of the few liqueurs that has never really been successfully copied, for its flavours are very subtle. Our recipe, although producing a very fine liqueur, falls short of the magnificence of Benedictine. If you don't believe us, go out and buy a bottle. Perhaps you can do better, in which case we shall be glad to hear from you.

## RECIPE 1

*Ingredients:*

360 ml (12 fl. oz.) 140° proof spirit
150 ml (5 fl. oz.) sugar syrup
2-3 teaspoonfuls T. Noirot Reverendine extract
Use a well balanced smooth golden wine to top up
This is 73° proof strength

## RECIPE 2

360 ml (12 fl. oz.) 140° proof spirit
120 ml (4 fl. oz.) sugar syrup
1-2 teaspoonfuls Vina Dictine essence
Use a well balanced smooth golden wine to top up
This is 74° proof strength

**RECIPE 3**

360 ml (12 fl. oz.) 140° proof spirit
180 ml (6 fl. oz.) sugar syrup
1 teaspoonful Semplex Dictine essence
Use a well balanced smooth golden wine to top up
This is 72° proof strength

# Chartreuse

This is the Queen of Liqueurs (the Kingship generally being attributed to Benedictine) and like most women of character it has subtlety, fire, enigma and passion in its make-up. It was originally made by the Carthusian monks in the monastery of La Grande Chartreuse near Grenoble, but when the monks were expelled from France they carried their secret with them to Spain and acquired a distillery near Tarragona. Nowadays it is made both in France and Spain, but the Spanish product is mainly reserved for Latin-American countries.

Chartreuse has a most complicated herb base, including angelica, balm leaves, hyssop, orange peel and many other ingredients. It is made in three types. Green at 96° proof, Yellow at 75° proof and a white variety which is stronger than the green, called "Elixir," which is unfortunately not now for sale. We feel we must repeat the legendary story of the little Carthusian monk, who, when asked the secret of monastic happiness, replied with a twinkling eye, "One third Green and two thirds Yellow."

**RECIPE 1**

*Ingredients:*

510 ml (17 fl. oz.) 140° proof spirit
210 ml (7 fl. oz.) sugar syrup
2 teaspoonfuls T. Noirot Green Convent extract
Top up with white wine
This is 92° proof strength and may require sweetening further
   according to taste

## RECIPE 2

**360 ml (12 fl. oz.) 140° proof spirit**
**180 ml (6 fl. oz.) sugar syrup**
**1 small tablespoonful Mixed Herbs "C."**
**Top up with wine of a golden colour**

*Method:*

The spirit and 240 ml (8 fl. oz.) of wine are placed in a container and the herbs are tied in a muslin bag and immersed in this mixture for four days, after which they are pressed and the mixture is poured into a bottle. The sugar syrup is then added and if necessary wine may be finally used to fill the bottle. If a golden wine is not available, yellow food colouring can be used to produce the true Yellow Liqueur type.


## RECIPE 3

*Ingredients:*

**390 ml (13 fl. oz.) 140° proof spirit**
**240 ml (8 fl. oz.) sugar syrup**
**2-3 teaspoonfuls T. Noirot Convent Yellow extract**
**Top up with a golden wine**
**This is 75° proof strength**


# Cherry Brandy

There are many fruit brandies, some made by distilling a fruit wine (i.e. Calvados distilled from Cider) and others by simply soaking fruit in Brandy. None of these has gained the popularity that is held by **Cherry Brandy** in this country (even before the youthful Prince of Wales felt the long arm of the law descend on him in 1963 while enjoying a quiet tipple). It is one of the cheapest liqueurs to make, and one which is unbelievably close to the original. Well matured elderberry wine (having lost its initial harshness) makes a splendid base for this liqueur. Cherry wine is also suitable, provided it has been made from deep coloured fruit.

## RECIPE 1

*Ingredients:*

**150 ml (5 fl. oz.) 140° proof spirit**
**150 ml (5 fl. oz.) sugar syrup**
**One teaspoonful Vina Cherry Brandy essence**
**Top up with Elderberry, Red Cherry or Bilberry wine**
**This is 44° proof strength**

## RECIPE 2

**150 ml (5 fl. oz.) 140° proof spirit**
**150 ml (5 fl. oz.) sugar syrup**
**1-2 teaspoonfuls Vina Cherry Brandy essence**
**Top up with a red grape concentrate wine**
**This is 44° proof spirit**
**It is best with this recipe to add only one teaspoonful of the essence at first, mix well and taste and then add the second teaspoonful only if additional flavour is required.**

## RECIPE 3

**150 ml (5 fl. oz.) 140° proof spirit**
**150 ml ( 5 fl. oz.) sugar syrup**
**2 teaspoonfuls T. Noirot Cherry Brandy extract**
**Top up with red wine, preferably elderberry**
**Add 2 ml (½ teaspoonful) citric acid**
**This is 44° proof spirit**

There are two main types of Cherry Brandy on the market, one is full-bodied and lush, similar to Recipes No.1 and No.2, and the other is full-bodied but fruity, more like Recipe No.3.

You can of course make Cherry Brandy this way:

## RECIPE 4

Take a jam jar and fill it with dark red cherries, which must be completely free from moulds, bruises or any form of decay. Each cherry is pierced with a fork several times before being dropped into the jar. Add 90 g (3 oz.) of castor sugar and top up the jar with cheap brandy. Cover the jar with a polythene cover held in place by an elastic band and leave for six months, after which it can be strained through muslin and is ready for drinking. In some cases a little additional sugar syrup may be needed according to taste.

This is a method which can be used, of course, for other fruits such as sloes, damsons, prunes or dates, and one can experiment with the home production of liqueurs in almost endless varieties and combinations. The high concentration of sugar and alcohol will prohibit fermentation, and all one is really doing is to flavour the chosen alcohol – it is worth experimenting, too, with vodka (which is itself tasteless) and gin – with the particular fruit or fruits employed. The method is extremely simple, if a little expensive.

# Cherry Liqueurs

We have already mentioned cherry brandy, there there are a great many cherry-based liqueurs, and many of them do not taste of cherries so much as cherry stones, which give a flavour rather akin to almonds. Kirsch, Maraschino and Ratafia are three of the best known in this category, but there are countless others, especially in Central Europe.

## RECIPE 1

*Ingredients:*

**390 ml (13 fl. oz.) 140° proof spirit**
**210 ml (7 fl. oz.) sugar syrup**
**1 teaspoonful Vina Kirsch essence**
**Top up with white wine**
**This is 75° proof strength**

## RECIPE 2

**270 ml (9 fl. oz.) 140° proof spirit**
**150 ml (5 fl. oz.) sugar syrup**
**2 teaspoonfuls T. Noirot Kirsch extract**
**Top up with white wine**
**This is 60° proof strength**

### RECIPE 3

240 ml (8 fl. oz.) 140° proof spirit
180 ml (6 fl. oz.) sugar syrup
1-2 teaspoonfuls Vina Kirsch essence
Top up with white wine
This is 55° proof strength

The addition of the essence can be made gradually until one's palate is satisfied.

### RECIPE 4

270 ml (9 fl. oz.) 140° proof spirit
180 ml (6 fl. oz.) sugar syrup
1 teaspoonful Vina Maraschino essence
Top up with white wine
This is 60° proof strength

# Cocoa

Moving into realms domestic, we may as well include a couple of recipes with a cocoa flavour. The well known liqueur in this range is called Creme de Cacao. It is very much an acquired taste.

### RECIPE 1

*Ingredients:*

180 ml (6 fl. oz.) 140° proof spirit
300 ml (10 fl. oz.) sugar syrup
1-2 teaspoonfuls T. Noirot Cacao extract
Top up with any wine
This is 43° proof strength

### RECIPE 2

150 ml (5 fl. oz.) 140° proof spirit
150 ml (5 fl. oz.) sugar syrup
1 teaspoonful Semplex Cacao essence
Top up with any wine
This is 43° proof strength

# Coffee Rum

While we are catering more for the female palate it is as well to mention the range of coffee liquers such as Tia Maria, Kahlua, etc. Drinks like these are quite easily made and we give a couple of recipes with a rum base which seems to blend itself well with coffee.

### RECIPE 1

Make 280 ml (½ pt.) of black coffee using a good blend of freshly ground coffee. While it is hot dissolve 225 g (½ lb.) of sugar in it. When it is cool, pour it into a wine bottle, straining it through a piece of muslin, and top up the bottle with rum. The flavour can be enhanced with one teaspoonful of Vina Coffee Rum flavour. This is 33° proof strength.

### RECIPE 2

**120 ml (4 fl. oz.) 140° proof spirit**
**270 ml (9 fl. oz.) sugar syrup**
**1 teaspoonful Semplex or Vina Coffee Rum essence**
**Top up with parsnip wine**
**This is 35° proof strength**

# Creme de Menthe

It is puzzling why Creme de Menthe is so popular. It tastes of chewing gum, or alternatively toothpaste, and the flavour stays in the mouth for hours. Ladies seem to adore it, and children (if they can get their hands on it when one's back is turned) like it even more. It does not seem to do them any harm; there is a great deal of rot still talked about alcoholism and the dangers of leading youth into bad habits.

It is interesting to note in this connection that scientists have discovered an enzyme called alcohol dehydrogenase which operates in the human liver and breaks up alcohol, rendering its toxic effect harmless. It would appear that some people's livers are deficient of this enzyme so that gradually a permanently toxic state develops and alcoholism ensues. From this it would appear that alcoholism may be a condition similar to diabetes and not a moral sin at all. It is hoped that when the enzyme has been isolated it can be administered to alcoholics just as insulin is to diabetics so that they will be able to live normal lives once more.

However, in case the children take to Creme de Menthe (taking care to top up the bottle to its former level with some of your wine) we append some low strength recipes.

## RECIPE 1
*Ingredients:*

90 ml (3 fl. oz.) 140° proof spirit
150 ml (5 fl. oz.) sugar syrup
1–2 teaspoonfuls T. Noirot Green Mint extract
Top up with a table wine
This is 35° proof strength

## RECIPE 2
*Ingredients:*

120 ml (4 fl. oz.) 140° proof spirit
210 ml (7 fl. oz.) sugar syrup
1 teaspoonful Vina Creme de Menthe flavour
Top up with a table wine
This is 37° proof strength

## RECIPE 3
*Ingredients:*

120 ml (4 fl. oz.) 140° proof spirit
270 ml (9 fl. oz.) sugar syrup
1–2 teaspoonfuls T. Noirot White Mint extract
Top up with white table wine
This is 35° proof strength

## RECIPE 4
*Ingredients:*

90 ml (3 fl. oz.) 140° proof spirit
180 ml (6 fl. oz.) sugar syrup
1 teaspoonful Semplex Creme de Menthe essence
Top up with white wine
This is 34° proof strength

# Drambuie

This is undoubtedly our finest liqueur. It is made in the Isle of Skye and is also called Prince Charles Edward's Liqueur. We would place it as the equal of Benedictine and Chartreuse, and like them is a herb based liqueur, herbs blended with honey and liqueur whisky. Tradition says that it was originally made for Bonnie Prince Charlie and that when he was rescued from his pursuers, with a few belongings other than the clothes he wore, his gratitude to his rescuers was such that he gave them the most precious thing he had, the secret recipe for his own liqueur. They have been making it ever since and it is now an established favourite South of the Border as well as in Scotland.

*Ingredients:*

**330 ml (11 fl. oz.) 140° proof spirit**
**150 ml (5 fl. oz.) sugar syrup**
**1 teaspoonful Via Honey Smoke flavour**
**Top up with a full bodied white wine, a grain wine possible**
**This is 69° proof strength**


# Kummel

The potato is a much-maligned vegetable. We must confess as winemakers that neither of the authors has ever made potato wine. In Ireland, of course, they make it and then distil it into a fiery spirit called poteen (pron. potcheen). When you drink it new you can go up five flights without ever touching the stairway. On the Continent they also distil potato wine and then flavour it with caraway seeds. The result is Kummel; just the thing for an English winter, but rather surprisingly it is still none too popular.

**RECIPE 1**

*Ingredients:*

**330 ml (11 fl. oz.) 140° proof spirit**
**150 ml (5 fl. oz.) sugar syrup**
**2 teaspoonfuls T. Noirot Kummel extract**
**Top up with low flavoured white wine**
**This is 69° proof strength**

**RECIPE 2**

*Ingredients:*

270 ml (9 fl. oz.) 140° proof spirit
120 ml (4 fl. oz.) sugar syrup
1 teaspoonful Semplex Kummel essence
Top up with white wine
This is 62° proof strength

# Goldwasser and Silberwasser

Centuries ago, when Europe was riddled with dreadful infections such as the bubonic plague, Gold, and to a lesser extent Silver, became the cure-all of the most unlikely conditions. Medicinal liqueurs were made containing gold leaf and silver leaf, and the most famous of these, Goldwasser de Lachs, was made in Danzig and is still obtainable today. Silver Water (Silberwasser) is not now sold in this country, but Goldwasser has considerable appeal, though the tiny flecks of gold-leaf are added purely for their attractiveness. Goldwasser has an aniseed base, and to this extent it resembles Pernod. Fermenta have prepared a T. Noirot Extract called Danzig which is complete with its gold leaf, and this liqueur generally proves fascinating to people when they first make its acquaintance.

*Ingredients:*

330 ml (11 fl. oz.) 140° proof spirit
120 ml (4 fl. oz.) sugar syrup
One bottle T. Noirot Danzig essence
Top up with as colourless a wine as possible
This is 70° proof strength

# Orange Liqueurs

Wherever oranges are grown, with all their variations, tangerines, mandarines, nartjkies, clementines, etc., liqueurs have been made using the peel of the fruit as a flavouring. Quite apart from the varieties of fruit there are degrees of ripeness and changes of basic spirit. As a result there is a whole range of liqueurs which collectively are known as Curacaos. They come in all colours — red, blue, white, pink and green, the colouring being mostly vegetable dyes (which incidentally are available to amateur winemakers through their usual suppliers). Here and there a Curacao has achieved such greatness that its name is greater than Curacao itself. **Cointreau** and **Grand Marnier** are two such names, while the South African liqueur Van der Hum (translated as "What's-his-name") is another but with a rum flavour in addition. In view of the fact that Curacaos are among the easiest liqueurs to make successfully, and liqueurs which with a variation of the basic wine achieve new and interesting flavours, we can recommend these as a good starting point, and include a number of recipes.

## RECIPE 1

*Ingredients:*

**210 ml (7 fl. oz) 140° proof spirit**
**150 ml (5 fl. oz.) sugar syrup**
**1 teaspoonful Vina or Vina Curacao flavour**
**Top up with fruity white wine**
**This is 52° proof strength**

## RECIPE 2

*Ingredients:*

**240 ml (8 fl. oz) 140° proof spirit**
**210 ml (7 fl. oz.) sugar syrup**
**1 teaspoonful Semplex Curacao essence**
**Top up with white wine**
**This is 54° proof strength**

## RECIPE 3

Carefully grate the peel of an unripe orange (in this country it amounts to an orange with small patches of green since a completely unripe one is not likely to be found). Soak this peel in 360 ml (12 oz.) 140° proof spirit for two days. Strain off and add 150 ml (5 fl. oz.) sugar syrup and top up with a fairly low flavoured wine such as carrot, birch sap, vine-leaf. Mix well and taste. At this stage add up to two teaspoonfuls of **Vina** Orange flavour little by little and tasting between additions. This produces a very full flavoured liqueur of about 73° proof strength.


## RECIPE 4

*Ingredients:*

270 ml (9 fl. oz) 140° proof spirit
150 ml (5 fl. oz.) sugar syrup
2–3 teaspoonfuls T. Noirot Curacao extract
Top up with Elderflower wine
This is 60° proof strength


## RECIPE 5

*Ingredients:*

150 ml (5 fl. oz) 140° proof spirit
150 ml (5 fl. oz.) sugar syrup
2–3 teaspoonfuls T. Noirot Orange extract
Top up with Orange or Lemon wine
This is 44° proof strength


## RECIPE 6

*Ingredients:*

180 ml (6 fl. oz) 140° proof spirit
60 ml (2 fl. oz.) sugar syrup
1 teaspoonful Semplex Orange essence
Top up with wine made from Seville oranges
This is 51° proof strength and is intended as an aperitif


## RECIPE 7

*Ingredients:*

300 ml (10 fl. oz) 140° proof spirit
120 ml (4 fl. oz.) sugar syrup
1–2 teaspoonfuls T. Noirot Mandarine extract
Top up with elderberry wine
This is 62° proof strength and particularly pleased our palate

# Peach Brandy

This liqueur is in our opinion better than Cherry Brandy, yet it has never acquired the same following.

*Ingredients:*

**270 ml (9 fl. oz.) 140° proof spirit**
**210 ml (7 fl. oz.) sugar syrup**
**2–3 teaspoonfuls Vina Peach Brandy extract**
**Top up with white wine (peach wine for preference)**
**This is 58° proof strength**

# Pineapple

Very occasionally in some wine merchants' catalogues there appears the liqueur Creme d'Ananas, a pineapple-flavoured alcoholic cordial. It is not very popular as a cordial, but with a little sugar only it makes an attractive liqueur, for the flavour blends very well with most of our white wines.

*Ingredients:*

**90 ml (3 fl. oz.) 140° proof spirit**
**120 ml (4 fl. oz.) sugar syrup**
**3 teaspoonfuls T. Noirot Ananas extract**
**Top up with white wine**
**This is 36° proof strength**

# Plum

If you ever go to Jugoslavia they give you Slivovitz to drink (local stuff which is anything up to 110° proof). If you are inexperienced you generally go blue in the face and the friendly Serbs thump you on the back until you recover, laughing merrily the while. Thereafter you are a welcome guest in one of the few Communist countries that does not regard you as a potential secret agent. Slivovitz is plum brandy, and while other blander plum brandies are made elsewhere in the world (Prunelle, Mirabelle, Quetsch, etc.) some of which taste of plums and some more of almonds, Slivovitz is the one that is spoken of in awe.

142

## RECIPE 1

*Ingredients:*

**330 ml (11 fl. oz.) 140° proof spirit**
**150 ml (5 fl. oz.) sugar syrup**
**2–3 teaspoonfuls T. Noirot Prunelle extract**
**Top up with wine (plum or damson if you have it)**
**This is 69° proof strength**

## RECIPE 2

*Ingredients:*

**330 ml (11 fl. oz.) 140° proof spirit**
**210 ml (7 fl. oz.) sugar syrup**
**2–3 teaspoonfuls T. Noirot Prunelle extract**
**Top up with light red wine**
**This is 66° proof strength**

If, in the above two recipes the sugar is lowered to only 30–60 ml (1 or 2 fl. oz.), and additional wine is used, in place something approaching a mild form of Slivovitz will result. It can be used as an excellent aperitif.

# Pomegranate

There is an alcoholic cordial called Grenadine which has a pomegranate base. Alcoholic cordials were much in vogue about a hundred years ago, but their low alcohol strength and over-sweetness make them rather unpopular today. Nevertheless Grenadine has a most interesting flavour, and one which blends very well with a young fruity wine, and although this extract was originally produced to improve indifferent wines, it can be made into a very pleasant fruit brandy.

## RECIPE 1

*Ingredients:*

**150 ml (5 fl. oz.) 140° proof spirit**
**150 ml (5 fl. oz.) sugar syrup**
**2–3 teaspoonfuls T. Noirot Grenadine extract**
**Top up with any fruit wine**
**This is 44° proof strength**

**RECIPE 2**

*Ingredients:*

    180 ml (6 fl. oz.) 140° proof spirit
    210 ml (7 fl. oz.) sugar syrup
    1 teaspoonful Semplex Grenadine essence
    2 g (½ teaspoonful) citric acid
    Top up with any wine
    This is 45° proof strength

# Punch

Most people think of Punch as a festive drink, but not as a liqueur. In actual fact there are several liqueurs called Punch. Down in the West Country there is a liqueur made at Burnham-on-Sea called Olde Exmoor Punch. It is a delightful refreshing liqueur and ought to be much better known.

*Ingredients:*

    120 ml (4 fl. oz.) Rose's Lime Juice.
    450 ml (15 fl. oz.) Brandy.
    210 ml (7 fl. oz.) Rum.
    3 teaspoonsfuls T. Noirot Punch extract.

*Method:*

The extract should be added a little at a time until the required taste has been achieved. This is 58° proof strength.

# Sloe Gin

For this one recipe we return to the ancient tradition of this country and give a method known to our grandmothers and theirs before them.

Fill a jar with fresh, ripe sloes (discarding any that show signs of damage or mould). Each sloe must be pricked a few times with a fork. Add 300 g (10 oz.) sugar to each 450 g (1 lb.) of sloes. Leave for 10 days and then fill the jar up with gin. The jar should then be sealed for 2–3 months, and inverted from time to time, after which the liquor should be strained off and bottled.

# Strega

This is the proprietary name of a famous Italian liqueur. Strega means "witch" for it is said to have a bewitching effect, and rates high in the armoury of love potions. Like many of the highest ranking liqueurs it is herb based, and its exact composition is a closely guarded secret.

Take a large jam jar or similar receptacle, capable of holding a bottle of wine, and into it put 300 ml (10 fl. oz.) of white wine, 360 ml (12 fl. oz.) of 140° proof spirit. Take one small tablespoonful (slightly below level) of Mixed Herbs "S", tied in a small muslin bag and infuse this in the mixture for four days. Press out, pour into the bottle and top up with 150 ml (5–6 fl. oz.) sugar syrup to taste. A slight haze may on occasions be apparent which can be removed by fining or filtering, or by leaving the liqueur to clear naturally.

# Vermouth

When one of the authors was in Palestine during World War II, he used to assist in the vineyard and in the winery of the French Trappist monastery of Latrun. It was a pleasant way of passing week-ends and leaves, the quality of wine was excellent, and a great deal was discovered about the importance of cleanliness in the winery and the endless battle which has to be fought against hostile bacteria.

The quality of the monks' wine was such that orders came from officers messes as far away as Egypt, Syria and the Lebanon. Now the Trappists, as unpaid workers labouring from first light to dusk, attempted to do everything to perfection, purely for the greater glory of God. Most of the surplus wealth derived from wine sales was spent on alleviating the poverty among the local people. Nevertheless, even with such dedication the attempt to increase output to cope with the apparent endless thirst of the British resulted in an occasional small batch of wine being "spoiled." The spoilage might consist of a mild bacterial infection but more commonly arose from oxidation. These wines were converted into Vermouth and were generally drunk with gin.

The origin of the word Vermouth is in the principal herb used to flavour these wines, namely Wormwood. Wormwood (Artemisia absinthium) has been valued medicinally for hundreds of years for its anthelmintic value and as a general tonic for weak stomachs. It is also a very good preservative, equal to hops, and has therefore been added to meads, cordials and wines for centuries. It is a very bitter herb and other herbs have been added to it to modify its flavour. It is the combination of these which form the basis of vermouth.

Other herbs used are balm, yarrow, chamomile, cloves, nutmeg, coriander, gentian and thyme. For those winemakers intent on building their own recipes we would refer them to "The Chemistry and Technology of Wine and Liqueurs" by K.H. Herstein and M.B. Jacobs, published by Chapman and Hall Ltd.

For most winemakers, however, it is fortunate that many of our main winemaking suppliers supply packets of vermouth herbs for both French and Italian Vermouth. The basic process is to make a small cotton bag, fill it with the herbs and then to attach a piece of cotton to it and to poke the bag through the opening of a gallon jar, holding the cotton in place with the bung. Each day for a few days the bag is swirled around the wine in the jar until enough flavour has been extracted, after which the bag is removed and wine allowed to mature slightly and clear. This latter clarification process is the most difficult since many of the herbs used impart a slight "moonstone" type of haze which is very difficult to dispose of except by filtration. To combat this it is preferable to stuff one's cotton bag of herbs into a medicine bottle and to pour on a mixture of one's strongest wine with a miniature vodka or brandy. The extraction process is very much quicker, taking perhaps two days only at normal temperatures, following which the essence is decanted off into the wine with little risk of haze.

Winemakers will have realised that the principal problem is achieving the degree of flavour desired by them. This is slightly complicated by the flavour of the wine being treated and the fact that the vermouth flavour diminishes with time. We have found that a vermouth kept for two years had lost so much of its original flavour as to be no longer recognisable as vermouth. It is better therefore to slightly overflavour and to store the wine in bottle for a couple of months before drinking it. If by some chance excessive vermouth flavour has been imparted, this is easily remedied by diluting the flavour with more wine.

In conclusion, while the purpose of this chapter is to provide a drinkable wine, mainly as an aperitif, from what would otherwise be a winemaker's failure, there is a small band of vermouth connoisseurs in the world who will no doubt concoct their own mixtures of herbs for infusion. We would remind these winemakers that commercial vermouths are generally around 18–20% alcohol by volume (roughly 30–35° Proof) so that any worthy achievement in this field could be crowned by a little judicious fortification.

We hope that this little adventure into the world of liqueurs and aperitifs will have proved interesting, and that you will venture further yourselves. It is such an individual world that you will be doing more or less what your ancestors did hundreds of years back. Trial and error is the essence of this art. What few rules there are, have been described. Some of the essences can be blended themselves with advantage, but this leap in the dark is your privilege. Your own wines provide another variable element, so that you may stumble on some new flavour or bouquet. We wish you good luck in your attempts.

# INDEX

## Other "AW" Books

### SEND FOR OUR CURRENT PRICE LIST

### J. R Mitchell
### SCIENTIFIC WINEMAKING–MADE EASY

–this is the book that every serious and ambitious winemaker has been waiting for; it is easily the most advanced yet down-to-earth manual available. It deals in detail with the chemistry of wine, but it also sets out for you a wealth of valuable information. It has a wonderful chapter of detailed recipes for making specific types of fruit wines, and another excellent one on the simple tests that a winemaker can use to ensure wines of perfect balance and highest quality. Written by a scientist who specialises in quality control, it will open your eyes to the possibilities of improvement that a little scientific knowledge can bring to your winemaking. 260 pages.

**Ken Shales**
## BREWING BETTER BEERS

—a lively paperback on home brewing by a real master of the craft, Ken Shales, of Basildon (which is likely to be renamed Boozledon from now on, it seems!) This book gives Ken's personal, well-tried recipes for all types of malt liquor from lightest lager to blackest double-stout and explains many finer points of brewing technique. A book no really thirsty home brewer should be without!

**C. J. J. Berry**
## WINEMAKING WITH CANNED AND DRIED FRUIT

—the simplest, most convenient and most economical of all. How to make delightful wines from the ready-prepared ingredients you can find at your grocers or supermarket, tinned fruits and juices, pulps, purees, pie fillings, concentrates, jams, jellies and dried fruit.

**C. J. J. Berry**
## FIRST STEPS IN WINEMAKING

—the acknowledged introduction to the subject; acclaimed by thousands (over 2 million have already been sold). Unbeatable at the price; winemaking clearly explained, over 150 reliable recipes, using the hydrometer; mead; cider; perry; judging; exhibiting. Illustrated.

**C. J. J. Berry**
## 130 NEW WINEMAKING RECIPES

—the companion paperback to *First Steps*, augmenting its 150 recipes with 130 others using newly available ingredients. Together these two books give you a unique collection of up-to-date recipes. It is also a complete instruction book in itself. Illustrations, and 50 amusing cartoons by Rex Royle.

**C. J. J. Berry**
## HINTS ON HOME BREWING

—concise and well-illustrated "rapid course" for home brewers, containing all the basic, down-to-earth essentials.

Send S.A.E. for our up to date price list

**Edited C. J. J. Berry**
**"AMATEUR WINEMAKER" RECIPES**

–this useful AW paperback contains a fascinatingly varied collection of over 200 recipes garnered from several years' issues of the winemaker's favourite magazine. They include many by that well-known Birmingham winemaker Cyril Shave, a specialist in wines from herbs, and a particularly useful set of recipes for liqueurs, punches, mulls, fruit cups and other party drinks. The cartoons are by Rex Royle.

**C. J. J. Berry**
**HOME BREWED BEERS AND STOUTS**

–the very first full-length book on this fascinating subject to be published, and still the best; many thousands of copies have been sold. Bang up-to date, it covers: The story of ale and beer; Types of beer and stout; Background to brewing; Brewing at home from barley, malt, malt extract, dried malt extract, other herbs and grits; How to make lager, pale ale, light, mild, brown, bitter, stout, barley wine, mock beers. Well illustrated.

**Dave Line**
**BEER KITS AND BREWING**

–Information on beer kits, hopped worts, malt extraction and new equipment. Pressure barrels and injector systems. Illustrated, 50 new exciting recipes.

**Peter McCall**
**DIABETIC BREWING AND WINEMAKING**

–is it safe? How much? Can a Diabetic brew beer and wine? All the answers plus many recipes.

**J. Restall and D. Hebbs**
**HOW TO MAKE WINES WITH A SPARKLE**

–John Restall and Don Hebbs have spent years exploring the techniques of sparkling wine production and in discovering the secrets of producing champagne-like wine of superb quality. Produce impressive sparkling wines which will be the envy and admiration of your winemaking friends.

Send S.A.E. for our up to date price list

**Bryan Acton**
## RECIPES FOR PRIZEWINNING WINES

–recipes for making your own wines are not difficult to come by nowadays: recipes which will produce *quality* wines are. That is where this book can help you. Most of the recipes that it contains have won prizes in national and regional shows, and they have been garnered over several years by Bryan Acton; others have been devised by him to guarantee first-class results.

**Ken Shales**
## ADVANCED HOME BREWING

–the next step from "Brewing Better Beers". This second book is the most advanced one on home brewing available in Great Britain. In it Ken reviews the various ingredients used in brewing and gives his personal recipes for a wide range of popular beers and stouts. Contains much information which is not to be found else-where.

**Bryan Acton and Peter Duncan**
## MAKING MEAD

–the up-to-date approach to man's most ancient drink. How to make meads (sweet and dry), melomels, hyppocras, metheglin, pyments, cyser, etc., etc. The only full-length paperback on this winemaking speciality available.

**P. Duncan and B. Acton**
## PROGRESSIVE WINEMAKING

–this magnificent, fact-packed volume by these two well-known wine-making experts has been hailed as one of the best books of the decade; it deals with advanced winemaking in a readable way, and carries its erudition lightly. This really fat volume–500 pages–is really two books in one. Part I dealing with the scientific theory of winemaking, sulphite, acidity, tannin, water, the hydrometer, the meaning of pH, yeast nutrients, preparation of the must, fermentation, racking, clarification, continuous filtering, building a press, blending, fortification, wine disorders, etc. Part II deals with the production of quality wines.

Send S.A.E. for our up to date price list

**C. J. Dart and D. A. Smith**
**WOODWORK FOR WINEMAKERS**

–have you ever wanted to make your own wine press? Or fruit pulper? Or winery? If you have, then this is the book for you. It explains how over thirty useful pieces of winemaking equipment can be made easily and cheaply at home using only the most elementary tools. The authors give clear and detailed working drawings and instructions in every case.

**Jo Deal**
**MAKING CIDER**

–In "Making Cider", Jo Deal, whose interest in cider was aroused in 1970 when she moved to Devon from Harrow, tells something of the history of cider, describes commercial cider making, and advises as to the types of apple to use, lists the equipment necessary, goes into cidermaking techniques with particular reference to acidity, pectin, yeast, fermenting and bottling. Gives recipes for sparkling, dry, sweet, "country", Devon, and instant ciders.

**S.W. (Andy) Andrews**
**BE A WINE AND BEER JUDGE**

–there are many proficient winemakers, and perhaps exhibitors who have toyed with the idea of becoming an officially recognised wine judge, but just do not know where to start, or how to qualify. This book tells them how.

**Wilf Newsom**
**THE HAPPY BREWER**

–Caters for the home brewer who wishes to go more deeply into the theory of brewing.

**Anne Parrack**
**COMMONSENSE WINEMAKING**

–A practical no frills primer in winemaking and with its aid anyone can quickly and easily be making superb wines.

Send S.A.E. for our up to date price list

**Roy Ekins**
**WORLDWIDE WINEMAKING RECIPES**
–An intriguing book of recipes ranging from prickly pears to paw paws to lychees and logans.

**Dave Line**
**BREWING BEERS LIKE THOSE YOU BUY**
–Over 100 original recipes to enable you to initiate famous beers from around the world. Full instructions for the beginner.

**Dave Line**
**THE BIG BOOK OF BREWING**
–the book which has become the definitive one on how to make beers of superb quality by the mashing method used for all true beers. It details an easy method of controlling the temperature throughout the mashing period. Fully illustrated.

Send S.A.E. for our up to date price list

If you have enjoyed this book
you will find equally useful its
companion volume

# "FIRST STEPS IN WINEMAKING"

by C. J. J. Berry

Full but concise technical information:
winemaking made easy; how to use
the hydrometer; **130 recipes for
popular wines;** making cider and mead,
etc., etc.

from

**Amateur Winemaker Publications**

**Argus Books Limited**
**Wolsey House, Wolsey Road,**
**Hemel Hempstead, Herts. HP2 4SS**